Clear Vision

HOW THE BIBLE TEACHES US TO
VIEW THE WORLD

Andy Daniell, Ph.D.

Deep River
B O O K S

Clear Vision: How the Bible Teaches Us to View the World

© 2017 by Andy Daniell
Published by Deep River Books
Sisters, Oregon
www.deepriverbooks.com

ISBN – 13: 9781632694560
Library of Congress Cataloging-in-Publication Data 2017947397

Printed in the USA
2017—First Edition
26 25 24 23 22 21 20 19 18 17   10 9 8 7 6 5 4 3 2 1

Cover design by Joe Bailen, Contajus Designs

At the end of the preface to the revised edition of his book *The Aquariums of Pyongyang*, Kang Chol-hwan closed with a call to prayer for his homeland of North Korea:

> Lastly, I invite all of us to an unceasing prayer vigil for the early departed and for a hastened liberation followed by true democracy in my homeland.[1]

I open this book with a renewed invitation to an unceasing prayer vigil for the people of North Korea.

---

[1] Kang Chol-Hwan, *The Aquariums of Pyongyang* (New York: Basic Books, 2005), xiii.

Contents

Introduction

A member of my church walked up to me one night and said, "My wife and I are thinking about reading /working through John Gottman's relationship book *The Seven Principles for Making Marriage Work*. In looking into the subject, we see that he is widely regarded as the foremost academic expert in the United States on relationships, especially the marriage relationship. We just wondered how his recommendations match up with what the Bible teaches on the subject."

Without having to do much research, I quickly found out that Dr. Gottman's main findings square perfectly with what is known as the biblical worldview. He has found, through his studies, that whether a couple takes a break in an argument is the single best predictor of how likely the marriage is to survive. When I read that summary of his work I immediately said to myself, "That is the lesson of Proverbs 17:14 in the Bible. That verse has been included in every marriage seminar I have ever been involved in at a church." Gottman also speaks in his book about how we have to be careful in a marriage in starting off our arguments too gruffly (avoiding "harsh start-ups," he calls it). Of course, that made me think of Proverbs 15:1–4. Those verses, too, have also been used in every church marriage seminar since Solomon was king of Israel. Dr. Gottman did not take the material for his books directly from the Bible (it comes from his decades of academic research), but the conclusions he reaches agree perfectly with the Bible's teachings.

Interestingly, at a different time, a young mother asked me about the book *Raising an Emotionally Intelligent Child* by the same author. She had encountered the concept of emotional intelligence (EQ), and understood that a high EQ was more important for success than a high

IQ. But she had also heard the horror stories of some more experienced mothers, and the bad advice they had received in questionable books written by crackpot authors in the past. She knew that those previous guides to raising children failed because they were not in line with the Scriptures. She simply wanted to make sure that any resources she relied upon would coincide with the truth of what was taught in the Bible. She was not concerned whether the author was a Christian and pulled his information directly from the Bible (though she was a big fan of Dr. Kevin Leman's books for exactly those reasons), but only wanted to make sure that she did not reference material that directly opposed what the Scriptures taught.

Again, a cursory look at the subject matter immediately confirmed that this researcher's findings were also supported by the Bible. The summary of the book's main is, "It's important for children to under-stand that their feelings are not the problem, their misbehavior is."[2] As I read that, I thought to myself, "That is an almost word-for-word quote of how a Bible teacher I once had in middle school described what is meant by the Scriptures in Ephesians 4:26–27." Two thousand years before anyone had ever heard of emotional intelligence, the apostle Paul had written—in what became the letter of Ephesians in the Bible—that strong emotions may not be sinful, but that we have to be on guard not to let them lead us to sinful actions. Those verses further warned that these sinful reactions can come in two forms—immediate negative reac-tions, and those that become bad habits or addictions over time. And the biblical idea of not letting strong emotions lead us into sinful behav-iors is really three thousand years old—as Paul was obviously drawing from the writings of David, a thousand years earlier, in Psalm 4:4–5.

Another example of modern-day research that aligns perfectly with the biblical worldview is summarized by Paul Tough in his book *How Children Succeed*. And I could list example after example of books,

---

[2] John Gottman, *Raising an Emotionally Intelligent Child* (New York: Simon & Schus-ter Paperbacks, 1997), 101.

academic research and worldwide "isms" that agree or disagree with the way the Bible says the world works.

It should be noted that a biblical worldview is not just what the Bible says is moral or immoral behavior. At its core, the biblical worldview answers the most fundamental questions of mankind:

- The ultimate *origin* of everything (including but not limited to humans and our morals)
- The ultimate *purpose* of everything (including but not limited to humans and our morals)
- The nature of God and the nature of man
- The beginning foundations of knowledge
- The framework we are to use in asking and answering questions to accumulate additional knowledge

The Bible has proven to be the most accurate and predictive text ever written. For those who have looked into the matter deeply enough, we begin to see that with its historical track record, the Bible is the first manuscript we should turn to in developing an understanding of the world and the people around us. Taking the biblical view of the world allows for many nonsense theories and destructive avenues in life to be avoided from the beginning.

One of the best examples of this involves Karl Marx's political and economic system called communism. The entire structural foundation of communism (and other similarly idealistic political and/or economic utopian systems) sent up a biblical red flag immediately. The details will be discussed in chapter 6 of this book, but the theory that people had been corrupted by the economic systems in which they were functioning—and that exposing them to the right system would allow these newly uncorrupted people to work together for the common good—is a concept foreign to the Scriptures. Of course, the Bible supports charity and the concept of those with material possessions helping out those in need (especially those who are in need through no fault of their own).

But many people are surprised when they discover what the actual biblical view is of human nature and the Bible's call for external incentives (economic, political, legal, etc.) to help govern that nature. There simply is no system which can be devised by man that will make everyone a good person, creating peace and eliminating poverty and violence. Any and all theories past, present, and future put forth by humans which take as their foundation that man is perfectible by other men—and only exists in an imperfect state at the moment because of the environment around him—is a theory doomed to failure, and one which will be opposed by those with a biblical worldview.

For those unfamiliar with the themes woven through the Bible from beginning to end, this may come as a surprise. Some students of history believe that the Christians involved with the formation and success of European capitalism and associated elements such as the so-called Protestant work ethic must have been believers who sold out their true beliefs for a monetary profit. But nothing could be further from the truth.

Another example where a theory opposed to the biblical worldview was almost immediately denounced by Christians was Freud's theories on psychology. I won't go into many specifics here; Jay Adams, in his book *Competent to Counsel*, does a good job of detailing where Freudian psychoanalysis broke from biblical teaching and why it essentially failed as a theory and let down so many patients subjected to it over the years. But the high-level reasons those with a biblical worldview rejected Freud was because he seemed to only blame mental illness on a false guilt brought on by the arbitrary restrictions others placed in someone's life (from which came all the famous cartoons of patients lying on the psychiatrist's couch complaining about their mothers). But the Bible teaches us that guilt can come from having violated real, absolute rights and wrongs, not just rights and wrongs that others made up and pushed upon us. The Bible also teaches us to look inside ourselves for the explanations of why we do wrong things, instead of looking for others to blame.

For decades, the opposing theories of Sigmund Freud and Carl Jung were fought over by academic psychiatrists and psychologists. Christians with a biblical worldview knew immediately that Jung's psychological theories would prove to be of much more value than Freud's. Today, tools based off of Jung's theories, such as the MBTI personality profiles, are some of the most respected and widely used in the academic and corporate worlds, while Freud's theories are mostly held in disregard—just as a biblical view of the two approaches suggested they should be and ultimately would be.

One of the most popular and effective methods used by psychologists today is called cognitive behavior therapy. This approach works to change an individual's destructive or irrational thoughts by having them think and act in ways counter to those negative thoughts until the new way of thinking and acting becomes ingrained—literally, until the connections in the brain associated with those thought patterns and associated actions have been "rewired." Patients who have used this methodology have overcome all types of phobias, irrational fears, and obsessive-compulsive disorders. The technique works primarily because of what neuroscientists call the plasticity of the brain. In other words, humans can train their brains to work differently (causing their actions to change in response) just by how they are instructed to think about certain areas of their lives.

Of course, the Bible taught us about this as well a couple of thousand years ago. In Romans 12 and Ephesians 4, the apostle Paul writes about being "transformed by the renewal of your mind" and being "renewed in the spirit of your minds"—literally creating a new self from the inside out. For the longest time, science did not agree with these statements. The scientific community claimed there was no "spirit of our minds" and that we could not transform ourselves into something different simply by renewing our minds. Today, however, with the discovery of neuroplasticity, the success of cognitive behavior therapy, and the introduction into the scientific community of books such as *Brain Rules*, *The Emotional Life of Your Brain* and *Switch on Your Brain*, science agrees that we can use our (non-physical) minds to change our physical brains and create a new self.

As the above examples demonstrate, a theory, application, or methodology does not have to be based (even partially) on Scripture, nor designed or promoted by Christians, to fit a biblical worldview. If something agrees with the tenets of how the Bible says the world works—whether or not those promoting it wanted it to or even understand that it does—then it is encompassed by the biblical worldview. In fact, a great deal of what science has discovered over the last few hundred years was documented by scientists (some atheist) working in strictly secular universities. But the discoveries themselves—things such as the earth being round and rotating on an axis, the existence of dinosaurs, etc.—were not only compatible with a biblical worldview but were predicted by the Bible long before science documented them. We will explore this further in chapter 2.

It is important, before we move into the heart of the book, to make sure that there is no misunderstanding of terms. I do not explain herein what folks with a spiritual, religious, or even "Christian" view of things might think about certain topics. Spiritual, religious, and even Christian people, as often as not, have their views of the world determined by their own internal feelings, desires, and shortcomings. This book is about the view of the world which comes from the pages of the Bible, with no additions or subtractions based on additional texts or the thoughts and creations of man.

Among Christian believers who use the Bible in some way, not all have a biblical worldview. Some denominations and their followers have what is called a more liberal view of the Bible, believing most of it to be merely symbolic and/or considering the creeds in and traditions of their denomination, or the statements of their religious leaders, to carry equal weight with the text of the Bible. Those with a biblical worldview hold that the historical portions of the Bible (Genesis through Esther in the Old Testament, the four Gospels, and the book of Acts in the New Testament) are accurate historical documents inspired by God which report literal historical facts. And even where the Bible uses figurative language (e.g., in the form of poetry in the book of Psalms) and symbolic language (e.g., in describing future events in certain prophecies), those passages are still to be used in influencing how we perceive and interact with the world.

The Bible claims that it is inspired of God and relevant to all areas of our lives. At the same time, it warns us of adding human wisdom, creeds, or traditions to its words. It has information about who we are, where we came from, why we exist, how we should think and act, and various ways to improve ourselves and gain greater understanding. It provides ways to determine its own accuracy, and asks those who believe in it to shape their entire worldview based upon it. Obviously, if someone does not believe that the Bible is truly inspired by God or views it as only a story of general themes about good and evil, they are not going to base their entire worldview on it.

For example, although the scientific research underlying his book *The Moral Molecule* fits well with a biblical worldview, Dr. Paul J. Zak makes a statement in the book directly about the Christian faith which is an incorrect but probably common view. Though an oversimplification of his research, the main theme of the book could be restated something like this: The chemical oxytocin is "the moral molecule" in our biological makeup, and when people hug each other—among other activities—this chemical is released in their bodies, creating a greater bond and sense of trust and community between them. Christians knew the end result of this lesson from the Bible thousands of years before science stumbled upon it. The books of the New Testament tell of Christians embracing one another, and at least five different times we are told to "greet each other with a holy kiss." The instruction to greet fellow Christians in this way was provided to us in letters written by the apostles. It is obvious that the writers were saying greeting one another in such a manner would be good for the bonding and unity of the community (especially because these early church communities were often made up of people of different races and social classes).

I have had the opportunity to work with a few Christian organizations which help young men with addiction issues transition from

prison back into society. When visiting these temporary housing facilities—whether to feed the gentlemen, assist with a Bible study, or just
attend a Narcotics Anonymous meeting with them as an encourage-
ment—there are always two requirements. Because all of these ministries are working to employ biblical methodologies, they require that
I hug all the men upon entering and leaving, and that I pray for them
while I am with them. Whether the science behind the "moral molecule" had ever been worked out or not, these recovery ministries know
that the Bible teaches that hugs and prayers are important, and that is
why they are part of their regular routine.

So the idea that hugging one another is good for community or the
concept that there are ways in which people can choose to act (such as
greeting with a hug) which can help to rewire them from the inside out
meshes with a biblical worldview. But when Dr. Zak steps into the area
of religion, he isn't quite on target any longer. At the end of a chapter,
he makes the assertion that sometimes preset ideas from fields such as
economics or religion can distort how oxytocin is supposed to work in
helping us adapt to our world. The preset ideas he says can be harmful
if they give us a greater sense of trust and community than is justified
in some circumstances. To make his point he repeats the story of a "religious" prison guard who helped a convicted rapist get parole because
the prisoner convinced the guard he'd found Jesus and amended his
behavior. The issue can be brought to light with a quote from his book.
He says "deeply religious people sometimes work so hard to see the good
in others, and to be attuned to the needs of others, that they fail to see
the warning signs."[3] Maybe some "religious" or "spiritual" people fit the
description quoted here but those with a biblical worldview certainly do
not. The gentleman ends the chapter questioning whether religion has
been a positive force relative to human behavior overtime. But if one is
going to ask such a sweeping question in a book, there should be a distinction made between the types of religious thought which come from
the minds of men and the very different lessons and conclusions of the

---

[3] Paul J. Zak, *The Moral Molecule* (New York: Dutton), 129.

worldview drawn exclusively from the Bible—a book which, as we will see in the coming chapters, simply could not have been put together by man alone.

This book is about the worldview of those who hold to the teachings of the Bible as the foundation of their understanding of the world and their role in it. For those who are only vaguely acquainted with the Bible or a biblical worldview, there is a tremendous amount of misunderstanding, which I hope this book can clear up.

While it will be necessary to touch on a defense of the existence of God in this book, that is not the main point. The purpose here is twofold:

i.   to show that the Bible is the main mechanism through which God revealed Himself; and

ii. explain how understanding this shapes one's view of the world.

The truth is, that is all a book such as this needs to do. Although the debate has been hijacked in recent years by a few outspoken critics (who carry on in a state resembling an emotional temper tantrum), the fact is that the world's most brilliant and intellectually honest minds have historically (and still do) believe that there must be a "god-like" force in existence. I am not saying that all of these individuals confessed the God of the Bible or claimed that Jesus Christ is Lord. But I am saying that the most credentialed thought leaders among scientists and philosophers know that there must be something god-like that explains what we see and how it acts in such a systematic way. We can each study the rational and scientific evidence that drove the great thinkers of logic, philosophy, and science to believe a god exists. But each of us should also make a personal effort to determine who this god is, whether and how he spoke to us, and the ways in which it should impact our lives if he did.

Before we go into all the details related to those last two sentences in the following chapters, let me provide an extremely high-level overview of the current and historical figures who believe in a "god" of some variety.

Most think Albert Einstein was the greatest scientist of the last century (many say the greatest ever), and he said very plainly and purposefully, "I am not an atheist."[4] Max Planck—the other towering figure of science over the last century, who did for microphysics (quantum theory) what Einstein did for macrophysics (relativity theory)—was a Christian who believed in the God of the Bible. And the only legitimate contender with Einstein for the title "greatest scientist ever," Isaac Newton, was also a devout believer in the God of the Bible.

The great Greek philosopher, Aristotle, believed in god in the sense of the unmoved mover or prime mover. Essentially, if a material universe with regular laws exists, something powerful and eternal must be responsible for it. The well-known philosopher Rene Descartes was a Christian who believed in the God of the Bible. Over the last few decades, the philosopher Anthony Flew, atheism's most prominent modern spokesman, came around to a belief in a divine god. He states in his book *There Is a God,* "In short, my discovery of the Divine has been a pilgrimage of reason and not of faith."[5]

Though I am a minister today, my pilgrimage has largely been one of reason, as opposed to what one might call faith. And Dr. Flew and I are not alone. Faith doesn't have anything to do with the belief that a powerful, creative god-like force must exist. As we will discuss in later chapters, the existence of noneternal, physical matter, the laws that govern it, and the fact that some of it sprang to biological life in a self-replicating way are perfectly sufficient to make the existence of "god" the default position. Science and logic have shown us that the starting point for all mankind should be "a god exists!" Therefore, the real questions are:

i.   Is the Bible *the* way that this god speaks to His creation?

ii. And if so recognized, do you choose to follow the Bible's instructions regarding your purpose, and to view the world through its

---

[4] George Sylvester Viereck, *Glimpses of the Great* (New York: The Macaulay Company, 1930), 372–373.
[5] Anthony Flew, *There Is a God* (New York: Harper Collins, 2007), 93.

lens? Not all who believe in God choose to follow Him, including the devil (James 2:19).

Authors writing on every subject under the sun take jabs at religion, in the process ending up (I suspect intentionally) misrepresenting the true biblical worldview. History has shown that the best way to attempt to discredit the Bible is to discredit some other religion or spiritual philosophy, in hopes that the baby gets thrown out with the bathwater. It is easy to reveal and pick on the shortcomings of the religions made by man. And I confess that we will do it a bit in this book as well. For the sake of accuracy and fairness, though, the biblical worldview and all that it encompasses should be detailed out (defended even), using modern information and examples relevant to our modern lives. This book intends to do exactly that.

It is certainly true that not everyone will agree that the Bible is what it claims to be, nor will all readers decide to adopt a biblical worldview. But because of the vast number of spiritual and religious options available in the world, and the intentional and unintentional misinformation spread about the Bible and those who take their worldview from it, a book such as this needed to be written.

CHAPTER 1

How the Bible Judges Itself and Teaches Us to Examine the World

The sixty-six books which comprise the Bible were written by more than three dozen authors, over a period of fifteen hundred or so years. But God said to the first prophet He chose to write His words for Him, Moses—who wrote the first five books of the Bible—that He knew humans would always want and need a way to determine what was truly from God versus what was made up by man. God clearly states in Deuteronomy 18 that the first and best way to tell whether a prophet, his words, and his religion are really from God is whether his prophecies or predictions come true.

> And if you say in your heart, "How may we know the word that the Lord has not spoken?"—when a prophet speaks in the name of the Lord, if the word does not come to pass or come true, that is a word that the Lord has not spoken; the prophet has spoken it presumptuously. You need not be afraid of him (Deut. 18:21–22).

Almost fifteen hundred years later, Jesus reiterates and expands on this same lesson, as captured in the Gospel of Matthew:

> Beware of false prophets, who come to you in sheep's clothing but inwardly are ravenous wolves (Matt. 7:15).

Predictions and descriptions which turn out to be false automatically and irrevocably identify false prophets, false religions, and false scripture. It is for this reason that we can immediately dismiss religions such as Jehovah's Witnesses, Seventh-Day Adventists, and the main religion of the Mayan people. They all (and in some cases, repeatedly) made predictions (specifically about the end of the world) that turned out not to be true. The Bible says then that we are to dismiss those prophets as presumptuous, and their religions as false.

The ability to explain things and make accurate predictions are the metrics by which the Bible judges itself, and the metrics by which it ultimately teaches us to examine other religious claims and even the world around us. God tells us the reason that what He relays to His prophets to be written down will always be an accurate explanation and the reason His predictions will always come true is simply because He knows the "end from the beginning and from ancient times things not yet done" (Isa. 46:10). In ancient times, it was mostly the Bible's accurate forecasts of events that were yet to happen in the future which ensured its credibility as *the* Word of God (examples to come in the next chapter).

The Bible also openly states that God will reveal Himself through the realm of nature (Job 38–41; Ps. 19:1, Rom. 1:19–20). Of course, we would expect that this would be done via the biblical explanations of nature, which predict scientific findings over time. As history unfolded, man developed increasingly sophisticated ways to uncover how the universe works. So in modern times, God defends the credibility of His word primarily through scientific predictions and explanations. But before humans could progress scientifically and technologically, we had to develop and employ what is today called the scientific method. This logical structure for theorizing explanations and testing them to see if they can make accurate predictions originally comes from the methodologies the Bible lays out for judging itself, and is the process it teaches us to use in evaluating the world around us. Bible-believers were instructed to be the first people to think rationally in this way—the first people to approach decision-making by eliminating failed hypotheses. It is this rational foundation upon which a biblical worldview is built, not feelings or emotions as is often assumed.

The development of the scientific method is credited to Francis Bacon. He was a believer in God, and a man who had studied the Bible in great detail. These facts no doubt influenced his desire to leave to science a method of verifiable empirical examination that mirrored the approach the Bible uses to judge itself. The Bible states that God is a God of order, and from that we would understand that the world around us should work in a systematically and ordered way. Starting in the first book of the Bible, Genesis, God promised that nature would continue to work in a regular manner that man could understand and even predict (Gen. 1:14; 8:22). These elements—in conjunction with the fact that God instructs man through the Bible to fill the earth, subdue it, and have dominion or rule over it as His stewards (Gen. 1:28)—must have all played a role in allowing Bacon to formulate his method. Atheist philosophers and people practicing non-Bible-based religions had never hit on the scientific method, as did the Bible-believing Bacon, because the idea that the world was regular and predictable and was supposed to be studied, uncovered, and mastered to satisfy their Creator was foreign to them. As discussed above, God wants us to uncover the complexity and elegance of the universe as a way to find Him. Rodney Stark expands on this concept in his brilliantly written book *How the West Won: The Neglected Story of The Triumph of Modernity.*

As we will see, God also knows that as we study the world we live in, we will come face to face with our limitations, and be forced to realize that the laws of nature are not all we need to understand who we are. Bacon soon realized—as every scientist has since (at least in their own mind)—that when you first begin to conduct experiments to explain nature, you feel as though you will be able to "explain God away" scientifically, but eventually understand that, just as God says, you end up essentially proving the need for something very god-like through the experimental scientific method. Bacon has a famous quote which can be translated something such as "a little science inclines a man's mind to atheism but a deep study of science brings his mind back around to religion."

Because we will come back around to the scientific method so often in this book—including when we discuss science's dirty little secret in chapter 6—I will very briefly and very simply explain the Baconian scientific method.

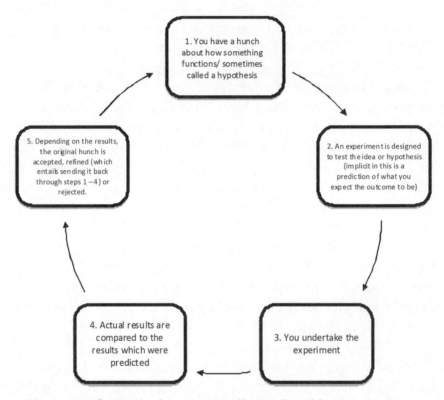

The Scientific Method, as Originally Outlined by Francis Bacon

For this process of investigation to work, the world has to be governed by regular, orderly laws of nature—which is exactly what the Bible declares. Of course, the method looks deceptively simple on paper, whereas in reality it can be painfully tedious, costly, and time-consuming. As a student of science and science history, my favorite part of the entire process is the designing of the experiment. The sheer genius and flashes of inspiration that have led to the testability of man's great hypotheses read as though they were a thrilling novel. Some of them—for example, Einstein's experiment to test his general theory of relativity's prediction about gravity bending light—require scientists to conduct experiments in extreme places and to take advantage of limited windows of opportunity. Other experimental designs—such as the search for the elementary particle called the Higgs-Boson, which had been predicted by certain theories in physics—take decades to come to fruition because of the immense cost and complexity of the experimental facilities which must be planned and constructed. In the case of the search for the Higgs-Boson, an entirely new facility was built—the Large Hadron Collider, which is essentially a seventeen-mile tunnel which cost a few billion dollars to put in place. Once scientists had agreed on how experiments must be designed and carried out to find the Higgs, it took ten years to actually build the large circular underground tunnel. From the original hypothesis about the existence of such a particle to the first experimental result from the collider which could be measured to verify it, the span of time was nearly five decades.

As Stark also outlines in his book, it is interesting to note that modern science with all its inventions and discoveries sprung from, and has really only been productive, in Bible-believing countries. Manmade philosophies and religions didn't predict the order of the universe and, therefore, never produced an environment conducive to large-scale, repetitive science. But using these (biblical) methods of explanation and prediction, humans have uncovered, documented, and even learned to manipulate and benefit from thousands of natural laws in our universe.

Two of the main issues for this book—in addition to the general understanding that the universe could be modeled in predictable ways—are: Which of the specific laws of nature were explained or predicted in the Bible and only later empirically documented by science? And, have any theories of science which oppose the teachings of the Bible ever been empirically validated as true? This is what we will investigate next.

Chapter 2

The Bible's Explanations and Predictions

As stated, the main element which causes human-proposed scientific hypotheses, as well as manmade religions and myths to be discarded, is that the explanations or predictions they provide turn out to be false. David Deutsch likes to use such examples in his lectures and includes a few in the first chapter of his book *The Beginning of Infinity*. He tells of the Greek and Nordic mythologies used to explain why the seasons change. Of course, those myths were replaced by the scientific explanation of the tilting of the earth, etc. In times past, when humans did not understand something, they would often make up a story (which frequently included gods of some sort) to explain what was happening and why. A desire to understand what is around us, and the need for routine and predictability in our lives, is common across all humans and has been for all time. Those with a biblical worldview, of course, are just as eager to discredit the myths and false religions germinated solely from human minds as are philosophers and scientists. Just because manmade religions turn out to be false does not mean that the Bible can be swept out with them. The Bible should stand on its own merits.

The Bible tells us that day and night and the seasons of the year will be consistent, but it does not explain the mechanism in control in that particular case (this, of course, as it should, set humans off in scientific pursuit of the answer). As we will see below, though, there are a great number of cases where the Bible does provide explanations or reveals natural facts, thousands of years in advance of humans using scientific techniques to discover them. And make no mistake, it is absolutely biblical that people would employ what we call science and technology to better understand, make use of, and live in the world around us. For example, when you combine the information in the verses Genesis 1:28 and Genesis 2:1, you can see that God is saying He has created once and for all everything that will exist in this universe (because the tense of the Hebrew word which is translated as "finished" or "completed" in those verses means "to be completed," "to be at an end," and "not to be added to or repeated"). God is tasking humans with discovering, rearranging, organizing and in other ways working with all that He has made, in order to release the creativity He built into us and to allow us to reach our full potential on the earth as we manage it. This is what is meant by the word in those verses that is translated as "subdue" in English.

The Bible lists out what today we call testable (scientific) hypothesis, and then encourages us to pursue knowledge over time so that we can look back and see how accurate God's Word is. Again, the accuracy of these testable explanations in the Bible—along with the historical predictions of the prophets which have all come true—is how God tells us to validate His Holy Scripture against all other manmade myths and scriptures.

The Bible, as with all communication involving humans, contains literal history, facts, poetic language, symbolism, certain commands, helpful suggestions, a little hyperbole and some humor. In addition to this, again as in everyday life, there are times when communication is meant to be educational/informational, but other times when it is only used in a way to move the dialogue forward. For example, a meteorologist might say on a newscast that the sun will be setting at 6:30 pm tomorrow. One could mistakenly believe this implies that the person forecasting the weather believes the sun is moving around the earth (because it can't "set" or "rise" if it isn't moving). That same meteorologist, though, if asked to give a lecture at a local school, would explain to the students that the sun is stationary with the earth spinning and revolving around it. What gives? Are meteorologists crazy or intentionally talking out of both sides of their mouths? Given our understanding of communication styles and uses, we all understand what is going on. A daily weather forecast is not meant to be a recurring lesson in science, it is meant to be a dialogue that aids our living our everyday lives in the most practical of ways. If I want to understand how weather systems work (as opposed to how they are going to impact my day tomorrow), I would rely on the meteorologist's scientific lectures, not the nonscientific phrases they use in their weather forecasts.

There are hundreds of books on fulfilled Bible prophecies, and some great reads on other amazing facts found in the Bible, from Henry Morris' comprehensive book *The Biblical Basis for Modern Science* to quick reads such as *Scientific Facts in the Bible* by Ray Comfort. Because the general understanding of what the Bible teaches is constant across those of us with a biblical worldview, these books all have many of the same examples and conclusions. The table below includes only twenty examples and is kept at a summary level. The examples are mainly taken from the portions of the Bible meant to be taken as literal historical and/or natural/scientific facts:

- The first eleven chapters of Genesis. These are not only meant to be read as literal history but are intended to be foundational books about what God created.

- The book of Job. In this book, Job suffers a number of tragic setbacks. As the story unfolds, Job's wife and his friends make various statements and judgments about what must be going on and why. At the beginning of chapter 38, God finally breaks in and speaks. God not only uses the events in which Job finds himself to help us see that we cannot fully comprehend God and His actions, but also intentionally uses statements of Job and His own proclamations to explain some natural (what we would call today scientific) observations. These chapters were intentionally designed by God to show His knowledge of His creation, in a way that would be testable over time.

- The writings of the major prophets, who set themselves up to be analyzed for accuracy by claiming to forecast events not destined to take place for hundreds of years.

Explanation or Prediction Revealed in the Bible	Subsequent Scientific or Historical Facts
1. The universe (matter, space, time) had a beginning. It is not eternal.— Genesis 1:1	Though they used to believe that the universe was eternal, scientists now say that the universe had a beginning and has not always existed. Common scientific ways to account for this are the Big Bang Theory or multiverse theory. Human thought, and therefore most manmade religions, have a view of nature processing in endless cycles. This is true for religions from the Eastern Hemisphere, such as Hinduism and its derivative Buddhism, to religions from the West such as that of the Mayan people, with its prediction that our world would end and enter a new phase at the culmination of a cyclical sequence on December 21, 2012. Many of history's most famous philosophers held that the universe simply must be eternal, because if it were not, something else would have to exist which brought our universe into existence. Logic dictates that if anything exists, then something must be eternal. That is, if the physical universe is real, then it has either eternally existed or it was put into place by something else. At some point in the train going backwards, however, there had to be a first cause—something that is eternal. It is a logical impossibility (the so-called *fallacy of infinite regression*) not to have something eternal (which did not require anything else to start it) to kick off the entire process. The Bible was the first and only source of information (religious, philosophical, or scientific) which has continually taught that the universe had a beginning (and will have an end).

Explanation or Prediction Revealed in the Bible	Subsequent Scientific or Historical Facts
2. God's promise of recurrence (and the fact He says He is a God of order) suggests He set the universe to run with machine-like regularity, meaning we should be able to discover and document laws about the workings of nature (though, because of how God created, not able to determine why those are the laws).—Genesis 1:28; 2:1; 8:22; 1 Corinthians 14:33	As mentioned above, until Francis Bacon, most of the world's intellectual elite did not systematically search for scientific properties and the natural laws that govern the universe because there was no reason (other than those given in the Bible) to believe that things ran systematically or could be understood in mathematical/scientific ways. On a related note, Einstein assumed there must be some creator because he was confounded at how precisely and systematically the universe worked. He felt the greatest mystery of all was that nature was governed by laws which could be studied and documented by man. Because we have all been raised in an era of ever-growing scientific study and documentation, we often lose sight of the fact that living in a world which can be studied and explained is a great mystery and a (nearly) impossible occurrence without some outside design. Einstein appears to be right—a creator/designer is needed to explain it all. As we discuss later, science is excellent at explaining what scientific laws are but not why they are what they are. This is exactly what we would expect from the biblical accounts.

Explanation or Prediction Revealed in the Bible	Subsequent Scientific or Historical Facts
3. Multiple verses (especially in the books of Job, Psalms, and Isaiah) speak of God "stretching" out the heavens at creation. This suggests that the universe was not created at its current size but was created at a smaller size and quickly expanded from there. It would suggest that if the universe is still expanding, it would be doing so at a slower rate than the initial expansion. This then would imply that light coming from objects at the edge of the universe would make it appear as if those objects were moving away from the center of the universe.	Scientists agree there was this rapid expansion of the universe. They call this cosmological inflation. This inflation period (which scientists believe lasted only a fraction of a second) would be needed to allow all the mass in the singular point before the Big Bang to achieve an escape velocity from the gravity which held it together. The problem for these theories is that there is no known energy source which could have initiated the Big Bang, nor given all the mass in the universe the inflation speed necessary to escape the gravitational forces. But an initial period of acceleration (called stretching out in the Bible and inflation by the cosmologists) is generally agreed upon by all at this point. Science has also documented a "redshift" in the light coming from the edge of the universe. This could be due to the ongoing expansion of the universe and/or the early time of initial stretching of the universe.
4. As discussed above, the tense of the verb used to tell us that God completed His creation also tells us that what was created could not be added to, subtracted from, or repeated.—Genesis 2:1	Science has discovered exactly what the Bible states here. Although matter and energy can be transferred from one state to the other (Einstein's famous $E=MC^2$), the total amount of matter/energy is fixed. This idea is not a hypothesis or some theory which needs ongoing testing to be validated. It is a fundamental scientific law known as the *First Law of Thermodynamics*.

Explanation or Prediction Revealed in the Bible	Subsequent Scientific or Historical Facts
5. The Bible states that the universe is "wearing out" and will eventually "perish."—Psalm 102:25–26; Isaiah 51:6; Hebrews 11:10–12	Science has proven that this is true as well. This finding is also a fundamental scientific law. It is known as the *Second Law of Thermodynamics*. This law states that every isolated system (such as the universe we live in) progresses into a less ordered state over time (scientists call this an increase in entropy). The implied consequence of this is that the universe will one day wear out and perish.
6. When combining the intentionality of God's having created life on earth in its various forms and the need for those existing life forms to reproduce in kind from the passages in Genesis 1 with the use of the verb already discussed from the first verse of Genesis 2, we see the Bible teaches that biological life does not spontaneously arise. Rather, it had to be created by God, and then can only exist if existing biological life reproduces that same type of biological life. Biological life is not a natural event which can happen at any time. It was a one-time miracle.	Science, of course, has proven this to be true. Biological life has not, does not, and cannot spontaneously arise from something that is not already alive. In the scientific research literature and text books this is known as the *Law of Biogenesis*. Biological life, in any of its current forms, does not just spring up out of nowhere, nor does dead material suddenly pop to life around us. Any new living creature is only given life by an existing living creature of the same kind. Of course, at some point, there had to be an initial living creature of every kind. Science has shown that new biological life only comes from existing biological life and how biological animals of various kinds reproduce. But science cannot explain (and will not be able to, given the Law of Biogenesis) how that first life naturally occurred.

Explanation or Prediction Revealed in the Bible	Subsequent Scientific or Historical Facts
7. According to the biblical story of the worldwide flood in the time of Noah, only a representative pair of each kind of animal was saved from the flood. But in all the later pages of the Bible, it speaks of the great diversity of animals that exist. The implication, therefore, is that there was a tremendous amount of diversity "built in" to each species.—Genesis 7–8	Humans have proven this to be true in agricultural fields, dog kennels, and in the scientific laboratory. Before Columbus came to the "new world," societies living in what is now Central and South America had used this built in biodiversity to breed different types of maize and potatoes from the original varieties that grew in their areas. The different types and sizes of dogs which were all bred from a common ancestor boggle the mind. We know now that this built in diversity comes in the form of the genetic code (dominant and recessive genes, etc.) unique to each kind of biological life. It is this built-in biodiversity the Bible alerts us to which allowed all the changes in the finches Darwin studied in the Galapagos Islands. It is this biodiversity upon which the forces of natural selection act.
8. The Bible clearly states, however, that while there may be a tremendous amount of diversity built into each type of animal, each kind of animal can only breed within that kind.—Genesis 1:20–25	Humans have known this to be true at least as long as we have had domesticated animals. Chickens cannot breed with pigs, which cannot breed with horses. This, of course, puts a severe limit on the functions of evolution. Natural selection can certainly cause giraffes with the longest necks to out breed and out survive those with shorter necks if food sources begin growing farther off the ground. But how does a frog evolve from a lizard or a salamander if salamanders can only breed with salamanders (which produce only other salamanders)? Scientific studies on the subject have been in agreement with the Bible and have shown this biblical declaration to be an insurmountable problem with the theory of evolution.

Explanation or Prediction Revealed in the Bible	Subsequent Scientific or Historical Facts
9. Based on the account of the flood in the time of Noah from the book of Genesis, we would expect the fossil record to show small creatures buried deepest in the hardened sediment, and larger creatures to be clumped together very near each other at the top of the sediment in the fossil record. —Genesis 7:11–24	The fossil record does indeed show that smaller creatures are buried deeper and that all large creatures are clumped together at the top of the sediment. Evolution predicts that small creatures would be buried at the bottom of the sediment but also predicts that larger creatures would be buried apart at increasingly greater distances (because it would take much longer for larger creatures to "evolve" into new large creatures and so more time passes between them existing and being available to be fossilized). This is absolutely not the case in reality! In fact, the fossil record documents what is called the Cambrian Explosion—all the fossils of large animals being clumped together at the top of the sediment, verifying that they were all on the earth at the same time and did not evolve separately over hundreds of millions of years. In an attempt to reconcile these hard facts with the theory of microevolution, the most absurd hypothesis in modern science was proposed—the theory of punctuated equilibrium. It should be noted that the theory of evolution also predicts that there will be hundreds of millions of "intermediate" animal species fossilized in between the layers that contain all the types of animals that we see on the earth today (in fact, it is *the* main prediction of microevolution relative to the fossil record). A frog did not just pop out a salamander egg one day. According to microevolution, there would have been

Explanation or Prediction Revealed in the Bible	Subsequent Scientific or Historical Facts
	hundreds (or thousands or millions) of creatures that were something between a salamander and a frog before the frog species that we know today were finalized. And that process was supposedly repeated for every living plant and animal that has ever existed. If this were true, then it would predict that the fossil record would contain more "intermediate" findings of fossils than it would of the distinct types of animals that we know today. The reality is, however, that there has *never* been a single true intermediate fossil found (they don't call them "missing links" for nothing). The Bible, of course, would predict that there would be no "missing link" fossils to unearth.
10. The Bible speaks about the earth being round and it appearing as a circle or a sphere from where God is enthroned.—Isaiah 40: 22	After assuming for centuries that the earth was flat (because it appears as such from where we stand on it), science finally caught up with the Bible and discovered that the earth is, in fact, round and that it looks like a sphere from outer space.
11. In an amazing verse in Job 26:7, it is said of God that He "hangs the earth on nothing." The Bible taught from the beginning that the earth "floats" in space.	Of course, early scientists, great academic men, and philosophers all thought this was nonsense. But as has been the case in dozens and dozens of scientific facts, science eventually caught up to the Bible, realizing that the earth hangs on nothing and essentially floats in space due to gravitational forces.

Explanation or Prediction Revealed in the Bible	Subsequent Scientific or Historical Facts
12. Even more unbelievable is that the Bible tells us that the earth rotates—as clay on a potter's wheel is the example used. It goes further, stating that it is this turning which causes the features of the dawn to stand out like beautiful strands of color in a fine garment.—Job 38:12–14	Again, for century after century, the best-educated people felt as though this biblical clause was insane. Everyone believed that dawn and dusk occurred because the earth sat fixed and the sun rotated around it. But this biblical explanation turned out to be as true as all the other biblical explanations and predictions. Humans have always been able to see the beautiful streaks in the sky at dawn and dusk and those who looked not only at the sky but also in the Bible understood long before science confirmed it that the dawn and dusk skies were a result somehow of the earth turning around on an axis as clay on the potter's wheel.
13. At the end of the book of Job, God is admonishing Job and his friends that they simply do not have the understanding of the natural world that He does. Of course, what God reports to Job about how His creation works has been some of the most useful predictions for science to use in confirming the accuracy of the Bible. Job 38:35 states that voices can be carried on what is "sent forth" from lightning.	As scientific discoveries were made and documented about the electromagnetic spectrum, one of the findings was that a natural discharge of lightning is what we call radio waves. Radio waves are naturally "sent forth" from bolts of lightning. And, of course, we all now understand that voices can indeed be carried over radio waves!

Explanation or Prediction Revealed in the Bible	Subsequent Scientific or Historical Facts
14. By only putting a few verses in the Bible together, it was easy to see that the Bible was explaining the evaporation/rainfall cycle that exists on the earth. The Bible claimed that the water which flowed from the rivers into the ocean would not fill the oceans up because some of it would return back to the rivers by being brought forth out of the oceans and poured out on the earth through the form of rain coming out of the clouds. This was a remarkable (and again testable) scientific prediction in the Bible.—Ecclesiastes 1:7; 11:3; Amos 9:6	This is yet another example of where the Bible explanations predated man's scientific discoveries by thousands of years. As man's understanding of the natural world grew, though, ideas were pieced together around various topics such as river flow, rainfall, and the origin of clouds until a few hundred years ago. A complete theory of a closed hydrological cycle was finally put forth and successfully tested. Because we begin learning about this cycle now as students in elementary school, it sometimes fails to impress us that Scriptures written as far back as three thousand years ago were already explaining this phenomenon.

Explanation or Prediction Revealed in the Bible	Subsequent Scientific or Historical Facts
15. Going back to the book of Job, we also see God speak about the greatest and strongest animals of His creation, what God calls Behemoth (a land and/or swamp dweller) and Leviathan (an inhabitant of the oceans). These creatures are described as being huge and untamable. Though a vegetarian, the Behemoth is said to have bones like tubes of bronze and limbs like bars of iron. The animal's strength is noted by God and its tail is said to be like a large, stiff tree. Based on these verses, those with a biblical worldview always assumed that at some point in the past, there must have been on earth animals much larger than the elephants and hippopotamuses we see today.—Job 40:15–41:8	Again, for centuries the most learned of men thought that references to such fanciful creatures help prove that the Bible was mere myth as all other so called religious scriptures had proven to be. In 1841, though, scientists began to realize that some of the fossils which were beginning to be uncovered belonged to a distinct class of creatures which no longer existed on the earth. A scientist named Richard Owen gave these creatures a name that eventually became "dinosaur" in modern English. The Bible said that such giant creatures existed on land and in the sea and that is exactly what modern science has now confirmed. It is a shame that the name "dinosaur" (which means something like "terrible lizard") was the name with which these animals were labeled by science. I think Behemoth, with its 3,500-year head start, should have been chosen instead.

Explanation or Prediction Revealed in the Bible	Subsequent Scientific or Historical Facts
16. One of the fundamental tenets of the Bible is that a human is composed of a Spirit and a body. The Bible does not teach that we are biological robots, everything about us predetermined by the neural synapses in our heads. Instead, the Bible teaches that we control our thoughts, emotions, and desires from our minds and, though the thoughts of our minds interact with our brains, the mind is different from the physical organ we call the brain. In fact, the Bible teaches that the mind can literally transform our physical brain into something new and that our thoughts, emotions, and anxieties can impact the health of our physical bodies.— Proverbs 14:30, 17:22, 18:14; Ecclesiastes 12:7; Romans 12:2; Ephesians 4:23	One recent scientific finding that has really excited modern researchers is the empirical understanding (driven in large part by advances in functional magnetic resonance imaging techniques used on the brain) that the nonphysical "mind" does in fact transform the physical brain. As mentioned above, the scientific community did not always agree with the biblical idea of "being renewed in the spirit of our minds." Without the sophisticated instruments available today, it seemed as though the way our physical brains were wired was a predetermined and fixed destiny. For years, the brightest researchers could not bring themselves to consider the biblical notion that the brain could be "transformed," literally rewired. The discovery of neuroplasticity, however, has validated the Bible's teachings in this area and opened an exciting new branch of science and research. I listed above some of the best books to read in this area of study but it is worth listing them again here: *Brain Rules* *The Emotional Life of Your Brain* *Switch on Your Brain*.

Explanation or Prediction Revealed in the Bible	Subsequent Scientific or Historical Facts
17. Moving on to predictions about the future (the element which has tripped up other religions and their prophets), biblical prophets foretold that the Hebrew people would be taken captive for seventy years during the time of the Babylonian Empire. They were to be taken into captivity in Babylon by the Babylonians but released decades later, to return to and rebuild their homeland by the order of the Persian Empire and its king, Cyrus. The prophet Isaiah made the prediction of Cyrus releasing the captive Jews 150 years before the event occurred, before there was a Persian Empire and before Cyrus was ever born.— Isaiah 44:24–45:13; Jeremiah 25:1–14; 29:10	The Hebrews were indeed taken captive by king Nebuchadnezzar during the 70 years of the Babylonian Empire. The Babylonian Empire essentially began when they defeated the Assyrians in 609 BC and ended when they were conquered by the Medes and Persians in 539 BC After the Persians were in control, their leader Cyrus II issued a decree allowing the Hebrews to return to their homeland, just as the Bible foretold.

Explanation or Prediction Revealed in the Bible	Subsequent Scientific or Historical Facts
18. During the reign of the Babylonian Empire, the Bible predicted it would be replaced by the Persian Empire, which would be replaced by the Greek Empire, which would split into four parts, before being replaced by the Roman Empire (which would be in place when the Messiah came to earth).—Daniel 2:31–45; 7:1–7; 8:1–8	Historians differ slightly on the exact dates, but the Babylonian Empire was brought to an end after being conquered by the Medo-Persian Empire around 539 BC. The Persian Empire ruled the known world until it was conquered by Alexander the Great around 332–330 BC. After his death, the Greek Empire had to be split and governed in four parts. Around 63 BC, the Roman Empire took control and dominated the world, including the land of the former nation of Israel, through the birth of Jesus (the Messiah) and into the era of the development of the New Testament Christian churches.
19. According to a prophecy given to Daniel, the Messiah (also called the Anointed One, or the Christ) that God had been promising in the Old Testament Scriptures would come to earth, claim His Kingship, and then be killed between a timeframe beginning 483 years after a decree was issued to restore and rebuild Jerusalem and the destruction of the temple, which would be rebuilt during that timeframe. Scholars agree the dates for these events calculate out to the period between 26 AD and 70 AD.— Daniel 9:24–26	Though they differ on exact dates, all scholars agree that Jesus of Nazareth came on the scene in Jerusalem, was baptized (and immediately anointed by God), claimed to be the King of the Jews, and was killed—all between the years 26 and 33 AD.

Explanation or Prediction Revealed in the Bible	Subsequent Scientific or Historical Facts
20. As mentioned in the row above, Daniel had fore-casted that the Temple which was to be rebuilt would be destroyed sometime after the death of the Messiah. Jesus Himself said (around 30 AD) that the temple would be destroyed, with each stone liter-ally torn off the others, before all those in the current generation had passed away.—Daniel 9:26; Luke 21:5–6, 32	The temple in Jerusalem was completely destroyed in 70 AD by the Roman army, which had encamped around and ultimately destroyed the city of Jerusalem during a siege lasting from 66–70 AD. The temple was lit-erally torn stone from stone by the Roman soldiers—who later looked for gold that had melted into the cracks of the walls and foundation as the city and the temple were burned in the attack.

The earliest human philosophers, scientists, and religious individuals all had very similar ideas: They thought the universe was eternal, and that time was cyclical. They never dreamed that the universe was structured according to knowable, systematic, mathematical laws. In a nutshell, the Bible plainly and boldly stated that the universe was not eternal, that time had a beginning (and will have an end), and does not run in cycles, but rather that God had promised a predictable regularity in nature. Probably even more amazing than that, the Bible put down the earliest documentation of what science came to call the First and Second Laws of Thermodynamics.

The Bible intentionally set itself up to be highly testable in the facts and predictions it relays to us. Again, it states boldly that God created matter/energy in a supernatural way; and that while man was charged with studying it, subduing it, rearranging it, and creating from within it, neither man nor any other natural cause could add to or subtract from what God had created once and for all. Science has tested this, and proven it to be 100 percent accurate. This First Law of Thermo-dynamics is not just a theory or hypothesis that applies to earth or our galaxy—it is a universal law!

Another quite testable fact confidently asserted in the Scriptures is what came to be known as the Second Law of Thermodynamics. It is interesting to note this universal law slams the lid of Darwin's version of evolution (in fact, slams the lid hard and bolts it down fairly tight). It is entertaining, though sad, to listen to scientists try and explain their way out of this paradox.

Not only does the Bible say that matter and energy were one-time, supernatural creations but it also states that biological life is as well. The Law of Biogenesis has proven the Bible to be correct on this account. Science cannot (and will not be able to) create life from scratch.

Science has brought us many great things in the realms of aviation, medicine, and communications. Science has explained many of the great mysteries that mankind pondered over the centuries. And science has also clearly demonstrated that physical matter cannot be explained by natural forces, and that biological life cannot be explained by natural forces. We are forced, based on the best scientific knowledge of today, to realize that something outside the forces of nature—something outside any force or process known in the entire universe—put our universe in place and created the life that is within it. This will be more fully dis-cussed in chapter 6.

But it isn't just the testable scientific knowledge contained in the Bible that gives to it an all-encompassing importance. Whether it is philosophers or religious leaders of various sects, predicting the future has always proven impossible. Nothing has a track record of foreseeing the future reliably other than the Bible. As already mentioned, many religions—from the Mayans to Jehovah's Witnesses to Seventh-Day Adventists—have made predictions about the future, but they all failed.

The Bible would demand respect as an authority of divine origin if it had only provided us with the understanding it does of the natural world, or only provided us with the accurate predictions of the future. However, it contains both!

CHAPTER 3

A Modern-Day Summary of the Biblical Worldview

Before we get into the summary, it is appropriate that this chapter begins with a few comments related to how one must interpret the Bible in pulling a worldview from it. The first rule we must consider is to not go into the Bible seeking to justify our own preconceived notions of how the world works (and/or why it works that way). We are to search the Bible and "meditate" on it (see Josh. 1:8; Ps. 1:2; 119:15; 119:97). The Hindus and Buddhists were not the first or only religions to promote meditation as a calming, edifying process in life. Building a worldview, according to the Bible, means not only understanding its command-ments and what it says about who we are and why we are here, but also understanding what it is saying about our motives. A great example of this comes from back-to-back verses in Proverbs 26:

> Answer not a fool according to his folly,
>   lest you be like him yourself.
> Answer a fool according to his folly,
>   lest he be wise in his own eyes (Prov. 26:4–5).

What?

This type of Hebrew parallelism is common in the Bible. In these verses in Proverbs, one of the things God is telling us that there is not a hard-and-fast rule about whether or not we argue with or try to instruct someone who is being foolish or destructive in the way they live. God must be saying that it depends on the situation and the people involved. If you ask me "Should I be baptized now that I have confessed Jesus as

Lord?" I would say, "Yes, that is clearly what the Bible instructs you to do." But if you ask me, "Should I answer a fool according to his folly?" I would start by saying, "That depends." If you are also participating in the same folly and will come across as a hypocrite, then absolutely do not answer. If you are trying to harm the person or their reputation, get revenge, make yourself look better in front of others, or make yourself feel better inside, then do not. If you are answering or instructing someone for God's glory and are trying to improve their life from a motive of love, then you should.

It is also required that we use Scripture to interpret Scripture, refining passages against one another. This ensures that verses are not taken out of context. We can again use the verses in Proverbs 26 as an example. Throughout the pages of Proverbs, we are told about the righteous, the wise, the foolish, the scoffers, and the wicked. If we are instructed in Proverbs 26:4–5 to both answer and not answer a fool according to his folly, it is likely that part of the decision is related to whether that fool is closer to the wise-man side of the spectrum or the scoffer end of the spectrum. This is so because other verses in Proverbs tell us that giving advice to a wise man improves him and causes him to give us thanks, whereas giving unwanted advice to a scoffer or the wicked really won't change them at all and might even cause them to lash out at us.

Another example of using Scripture to interpret Scripture comes from the recorded sayings of Jesus in two different gospels:

> Go therefore and make disciples of all nations, baptizing them in the name of the Father and of the Son and of the Holy Spirit, teaching them to observe all that I have commanded you. And behold, I am with you always, to the end of the age (Matt. 28:19–20).

In that passage from Matthew, Jesus tells us to go and make disciples; and in a complimentary passage in the Gospel of Luke, Jesus tells us how we make disciples of others before we baptize and teach them:

> Then he said to them, "These are my words that I spoke to you while I was still with you, that everything written about me in the Law of Moses and the Prophets and the Psalms must be fulfilled." Then he opened their minds to understand the Scriptures, and said to them, "Thus it is written, that the Christ should suffer and on the third day rise from the dead, and that repentance and forgiveness of sins should be proclaimed in his name to all nations, beginning from Jerusalem" (Luke 24:44–47).

We read that Jesus wants us to make disciples for Him and baptize them and teach them in one passage, and we find out how to make those disciples (proclaiming repentance and forgiveness of sin in the name of Jesus Christ) in the other passage.

It is also important to define key words in Scripture by leveraging other scriptures related to that word. For example, the word "faith" has a common meaning to all of us, and can be looked up in the dictionary. But there is also a biblical definition of faith, drawn from verses such as Romans 4:18–21 and Hebrews 11:1. Biblical faith is believing that God can and will fulfill all His promises, even when we cannot see that those promises are currently in the process of being fulfilled. Similarly, in Hebrews 3:16–19, the writer uses "disobedience" and "unbelief" as interchangeable terms. Therefore, those with a biblical worldview say that believing in God means that we believe we are to be obedient to Him, and having faith in God means that we trust what He tells us will come true.

In building a biblical worldview, it is also critical to understand the context in which various scriptures were written. If a parenting book says "It is okay to ignore the child while it cries," we would definitely need a little context. If that is a general rule, or if they are saying when you hear your young child fall down hard it is okay to ignore their crying, that sounds like bad advice. But if that statement is made in a discussion of putting your child in time-out after they have walloped their younger sibling with a tennis racket, then it makes more sense. If your child hurts their younger brother and you punish them by making them sit in their room, the child may well start to cry out of anger or in trying to make you feel guilty so that you cease the punishment. In that case, the book may say, it is okay to ignore the child while it cries; you don't have to threaten them to stop crying, or bend to their will. Taken in context, that seems like solid parenting advice. Taken out of context or applied in a universal sense, that sounds like a way to get a visit from the Department of Child Services. Context is huge in interpreting the Bible, and passages can be taken out of context intentionally or unintentionally with equal harm.

While there are always drawbacks when we take a high-level overview of complicated material, we can begin to summarize the thousand-plus pages of the Bible with only a couple dozen main themes. As I explain how the Bible teaches us to view the world around us, I will provide Bible verses, to provide examples of where each theme comes from in Scripture. In some sense, though, the entire Bible teaches these themes and that is why I can state these ideas literally provide the foundation for the biblical worldview. A few of the points below flow directly from the information presented in the first two chapters. Therefore, no additional documentation will be given for those items.

1. *God (through Jesus) created everything and everything was created with the purpose of glorifying God.* The Bible states unequivocally that everything (including the Bible itself) is about God. If we are mistaken in this fact, it makes developing a true biblically driven worldview impossible. At the highest level, this is the beginning and end of a biblical worldview.

   • In the beginning, God created the heavens and the earth (Gen. 1:1).

- The heavens declare the glory of God, and the sky above proclaims his handiwork (Ps. 19:1).

- For by him all things were created, in heaven and on earth, visible and invisible, whether thrones or dominions or rulers or authorities—all things were created through him and for him (Col. 1:16).

- But in these last days he has spoken to us by his Son, whom he appointed the heir of all things, through whom also he created the world (Heb. 1:2).

We see the blessings that we are given, the acts of kindness God asks us to do for others, and even the death of Jesus for our sins all as being God-focused phenomena meant to glorify the Creator of the universe. As soon as we start to see anything from a human point of view instead of the God-focused, biblical worldview, we will be misguided in our thoughts and actions. Notice in the Bible how many times we are told that something is done for God's sake or for His glory. Even when humans benefit, we are told it is done for God's sake.

- He restores my soul. He leads me in paths of righteousness for his name's sake (Ps. 23:3).

- Remember not the sins of my youth or my transgressions; according to your steadfast love remember me, for the sake of your goodness, O Lord! (Ps. 25:7).

- For your name's sake, O Lord, pardon my guilt, for it is great (Ps. 25:11).

- [Jesus said,] "In the same way, let your light shine before others, so that they may see your good works and give glory to your Father who is in heaven" (Matt. 5:16).

In his book *Radical*, David Platt wonders how people would summarize the message of Christianity. He says that answers such as "that God loves me" or even "that God sent His Son, Jesus, to die for me" are unbiblical answers because they make Christianity all about us, and it is supposed to be all about God.

Dr. Platt and I likely would not agree on every fine point of theology, but I did like how he describes the message and meaning of the Bible: "God provides for me so that I can reveal His glory to all the people and to all the nations. Now God is the object of our faith, and Christianity centers around Him." He continues with this final thought: "We live in a church culture that has a dangerous tendency to disconnect the grace of God from the glory of God. And while the wonder of grace is worthy of our attention, if that grace is disconnected from its purpose, the result is a Christianity that centers on us and bypasses the heart of God." He says, restating what he has found in the Scriptures, that even the grace that provides for our salvation is not focused on us, because God saves us for the sake of His holy name. Platt writes, "God blesses His people with extravagant grace so they might extend His extravagant glory to all peoples on earth."[6]

In a similar fashion, Henry T. and Richard Blackaby write, in their devotion book *Experiencing God Day by Day*, "What you choose to focus on becomes the dominant influence in your life. You may be a Christian, but if your focus is always on your problems, your problems will determine the direction of your life. If your focus is on people, then people will determine what you think and do." They add, "When you choose to focus on Christ, you invite Him to take the most important position in your life as Counselor and Defender. Every time you face a new experience, you should turn to Christ for His interpretation."[7] Of course, we seek His interpretation in the Bible.

2. *The overarching purpose, then, of our individual lives is to glorify God.* The Bible says that we are about God, too. We were created for God's

---

[6] David Platt, *Radical* (Colorado Springs: Multnomah Books, 2010), 69–71.
[7] Henry T. Blackaby and Richard Blackaby, *Experiencing God Day by Day* (Nashville: B&H Publishing Group, 1998, 2006), 206.

glory, and we are to live to glorify Him with our lives and reveal His
glory to others.

- And call upon me in the day of trouble; and I will deliver you,
  and you shall glorify me (Ps. 50:15).

- I will say to the north, Give up, and to the south, Do not with-
  hold; bring my sons from afar and my daughters from the end of
  the earth, everyone who is called by my name, whom I created for
  my glory, whom I formed and made (Isa. 43:6–7).

- . . . the people whom I formed for myself that they might declare
  my praise (Isa. 43:21).

- So, whether you eat or drink, or whatever you do, do all to the
  glory of God (1 Cor. 10:31).

3. *We glorify God by allowing our lives to be changed and through our
   service to others.* Jesus told us that the two most important commandments in the Old Testament were to love God with all our
   being and to love other people as we love ourselves. The Bible
   gives us various instructions on how we do exactly that. When we
   come to know and understand the person of Jesus Christ, it should
   change who we want to be—and over time, also change who we
   actually are.

   Think about when two people meet each other and develop
   an ever-growing bond and friendship (and/or romantic relationship). As the connection and love between them strengthens,
   they find themselves interested in spending more time together,
   learning more about each other, and are willing to adapt certain
   things in their lives to please and support the other person. A
   growing relationship with Jesus is in many ways the same. As we
   learn about Him and decide to commit to Him, we desire to do
   things more like He does. We come to understand God the Father
   through the person of Jesus; others around us should then come
   to understand Jesus, at least in some small part, through us. Playing this role—which the Bible calls being a spokesperson or an

ambassador for God Himself—brings glory to the Father. As I decide to and succeed in sweeping away the sinful habits in my life (greed, selfishness, fits of anger, etc.), people can see more of Jesus reflected in me.

We are also taught that for God to be glorified with our lives, we must think about and support others. The Bible teaches us to especially care for those who are struggling through no fault of their own, and are unable in any significant way to take care of themselves. As we make conscious decisions day to day that benefit others, even if it costs us in the processes, God is glorified.

- You shall not take vengeance or bear a grudge against the sons of your own people, but you shall love your neighbor as yourself: I am the LORD (Lev. 19:18).

- You shall love the LORD your God with all your heart and with all your soul and with all your might (Deut. 6:5).

- In the same way, let your light shine before others, so that they may see your good works and give glory to your Father who is in heaven (Matt. 5:16).

- And he said to him, "You shall love the Lord your God with all your heart and with all your soul and with all your mind. This is the great and first commandment. And a second is like it: You shall love your neighbor as yourself" (Matt. 22:37–39).

- Therefore, we are ambassadors for Christ, God making his appeal through us. We implore you on behalf of Christ, be reconciled to God. For our sake he made him to be sin who knew no sin, so that in him we might become the righteousness of God (2 Cor. 5:20–21).

- Religion that is pure and undefiled before God, the Father, is this: to visit orphans and widows in their affliction, and to keep oneself unstained from the world (James 1:27).

4. *Religious texts and teachings are to be evaluated and validated on the success of their explanations and predictions.* This was the main focus

of chapter 1. The two main verses employed in reaching this conclusion were:

- Deuteronomy 18:21–22
- Matthew 7:15

5. *The beginning of our knowledge and wisdom comes from a healthy reverence for God and the Scriptures He had written down for us.* Once we have examined all the options and see the Bible for what it truly is, then we are to have an awe and respect for the God it reveals, and seek to learn from the writings He inspired. Though there is much for humans to learn, we have come to understand that if something disagrees with the Bible from the outset, that path of potential knowledge will turn out to be a dead end.

- The fear of the LORD is the beginning of wisdom; all those who practice it have a good understanding. His praise endures forever! (Ps. 111:10).
- The sum of your word is truth, and every one of your righteous rules endures forever (Ps. 119:160).
- The fear of the LORD is the beginning of knowledge; fools despise wisdom and instruction (Prov. 1:7).
- The fear of the LORD is the beginning of wisdom, and the knowledge of the Holy One is insight (Prov. 9:10).

6. *God's physical creation works in a consistent, systematic way that can be discovered.* As mentioned in chapter 2, the Bible calls on us to be creative like the God who made us, and to subdue the earth by leveraging the regularity of the natural laws with which God endowed the universe to systematically discover and accumulate knowledge (what we would today call science, medicine, technology, etc.). The Bible is very specific in directing us to subdue the earth and rule over it as God's "on-site managers," and in telling us that the natural world would follow regular patterns which we could come to understand. God would not tell us to subdue and have dominion over His creation if it were not possible. And we understand the reason those

things are even possible is because the universe works in a predictable way.

- And God said, "Let there be lights in the expanse of the heavens to separate the day from the night. And let them be for signs and for seasons, and for days and years" (Gen. 1:14).

- So God created man in his own image, in the image of God he created him; male and female he created them. And God blessed them. And God said to them, "Be fruitful and multiply and fill the earth and subdue it, and have dominion over the fish of the sea and over the birds of the heavens and over every living thing that moves on the earth" (Gen. 1:27–28).

- While the earth remains, seedtime and harvest, cold and heat, summer and winter, day and night, shall not cease (Gen. 8:22).

7. *Building off numbers 4, 5 and 6 above: As God's earthly stewards, we are to accumulate knowledge so we can continue to subdue the earth and have dominion over it. We do this through testing theories, options, and processes—keeping the ones which can predict and explain, and throwing out the ones proven to be false.*

8. *Though other animals are not, man is more than a physical being.* The Bible says that a human (also called a "soul") consists of a spirit and a physical body (the latter often referred to as "the flesh"). The two interact, with the spirit able to transform the physical brain. The spirit will outlast the physical body. The two are often at odds with each other.

- And the dust returns to the earth as it was, and the spirit returns to God who gave it (Eccl. 12:7).

- Watch and pray that you may not enter into temptation. The spirit indeed is willing, but the flesh is weak (Mark 14:38).

- Do not be conformed to this world, but be transformed by the renewal of your mind, that by testing you may discern what is the will of God, what is good and acceptable and perfect (Rom. 12:2).

- . . . and to be renewed in the spirit of your minds (Eph. 4:23).

9. *The requirements and instructions God provides for us to live by deal in absolute rights and wrongs and are best for us, ultimately allowing us the most abundant life. Satan's biggest lie is that there are no absolute rights and wrongs, and that God's rules are unfair and restrict our enjoying the best possible life.* A critical component of the biblical worldview is the understanding that the directions given to us in the Bible, while nonnegotiable, are not rules to make life miserable or test our endurance in the face of bitter unfairness but are instead directions based on perfect knowledge and absolute truth which bring us great benefit (even when we don't understand how that benefit is derived). God told Moses to tell the Hebrew people that long ago, and Jesus explicitly stated as much in His teachings as well (emphasis added):

- And now, Israel, what does the LORD your God require of you, but to fear the LORD your God, to walk in all his ways, to love him, to serve the LORD your God with all your heart and with all your soul, and to keep the commandments and statutes of the LORD, which I am commanding you today *for your good?* (Deut. 10:12–13).

- The thief comes only to steal and kill and destroy. I came that they may *have life and have it abundantly* (John 10:10).

    Every youth sponsor and teacher who has ever dealt with middle-school kids knows the verses from Deuteronomy 23:12–14. These verses cover rules and regulations given to the Hebrews after God had freed them from slavery in Egypt. The words written in the Old Testament were given by God to His people more than three thousand years ago. The verses literally say that when the Hebrew army was out in the field, they were to have a place outside their camp where they went to do "number two" (most translations of the Bible use the word "excrement," and most middle-school teachers use the word "poop"), and that they were to take a shovel with them so they could dig a hole to poop in and then they were to cover it up. (Seriously, look it up.) Verse 14 says that because God is with them in their military camps, those campsites must be holy. Today, with our knowledge that until World War II the overwhelming majority of deaths in war were caused by disease—and our understanding of how those diseases (especially illness related to E coli, and the likes of dysentery and cholera) were caused—we can clearly see what a huge advantage this rule would have been to the Hebrew warriors. But with no knowledge of bacteria, germs, etc., they could not have understood how this rule was such a tremendous benefit to their health and safety. They would have had to follow the regulation based on a faith that a God who loved them would only require things which, even though they might be hard to apply and live by, would only be for their ultimate benefit. Can you imagine how difficult it must have been when the edge of camp was more than a mile away, you were tired, and the enemy was lurking out on the boundary somewhere, to jump through such a hoop just to take a poop? But the more you truly believe in your heart that God's will is best for you, then the easier it becomes to live out your biblical worldview. If there was a Hebrew soldier back in the day who did not have this faith, I can hear the arguments now.

Soldier 1: "Oh dude, if you're going to do that, remember you need to go outside the camp and dig a hole."
Soldier 2: "Why would you say that?"
Soldier 1: "That's what God teaches us is best, so I really think you should do it."
Soldier 2: "Well, I know another guy who's not doing it, and God has not struck him dead yet. Plus, I am really tired."
Soldier 1: "I'm sorry that you're tired, and I know it seems like a difficult rule to follow, but I really do think it is best."
Soldier 2: "Why are you being so mean to me? How could you care so little about other people? If God loves me, why would He ask me to do something that's so hard to go along with, anyway? If following those religious rituals is important to you, then have at it. But they're not meant for everyone.

You need to learn to be more understanding and try to think about things from other people's point of view."

Soldier 1: "Well actually, I'm just going by the things God had written down for us. I truly do want what's best for you, but I think God knows what's best to a much greater degree than you and I do, so I always recommend following His guidance. I know I don't always feel like forgiving other people, or sticking up for those who are being taken advantage of by others, or telling the truth when it would be easier to tell a quick lie, but I try and do those things because they're part of what God says He wants, and I know in my heart that they'll be best for me—and everyone else too."

If you ask anyone today whether hundreds of thousands of soldiers marching together should just do number one or number two in the campsite they are all staying in, they would all say "No." Their main reason would be obvious: The unsanitary conditions this would create would cause diseases, which would be much more harmful than the enemy's weapons.

This example may seem a little silly and out of place, but it is actually a very serious and powerful illustration. God says in the Old Testament books of Psalms and Isaiah that He is above us, that His ways are not our ways, and that we cannot think the way that He does. We do understand the role that unsanitary conditions and the associated bacteria and viruses play in human illness today, but the Hebrew military certainly did not when God originally gave them the scoop on where to poop.

We can be just as certain that there are thousands of other things that we do not understand about why God asks us to live a certain way, and why He tells us not to think or do certain things that He calls sins. Are some of them difficult to live by? Absolutely. And do I understand exactly what the benefit of doing, or the horrible cost of not doing, everything that God commands or forbids? Not at all. But I have a faith that God's ways are always right and always best, and this faith has only been strengthened by the example of the bathroom rule in Deuteronomy and the hundreds of others like it in the Bible. Over time, God has allowed us to understand how some of His seemingly nitpicky, difficult-to-follow rules have actually provided tremendous benefit to His followers. It is interesting to note that the only real method we ever see the devil applying against humans in the Bible (starting with his conversation with Eve in the Garden of Eden, in Genesis 3:1–6) is to get into our minds and try and have us think that God's rules are unfair—and that therefore we should use our own logic, desires, or experience to figure out our own personal right from wrong. Our pride works against us when the devil tells us God's rules are unfair, our desire to be independent works against us, and the pressure of other people who say we are being thoughtless works against us and seeing people supposedly succeed in life who we know break God's rules works against us on this front. God is not really worried about whether people believe in a higher power; almost everyone on the planet does. But God is concerned that humans will see what He had written in the Bible as somehow not being one-hundred-percent best for us. Those with a biblical worldview understand that we should be looking to the Bible always and the Bible only for guidance—as opposed to going with our gut, our passions, or whatever feels good.

This idea that God asks us to behave in ways that we don't understand, or that don't seem fair or natural, is the root of sin today as well. For example, I have had a few men talk to me about them cheating on their wife or girlfriend as if they were fishing for my approval. In most cases they justify their behavior by saying something such as, "God made me with hormones and obviously created people to have sex. It is unnatural for people to just have one partner." They almost always say that they don't want to be bad people, and do not feel as though they are bad people, but just cannot see being faithful to only a single person for the rest of their lives. I think in these cases, the individuals are wanting me to explain to them exactly why the Bible says it is wrong, and exactly how it justifies limiting humans to only sexual activity inside a one-man, one-woman marriage. Of course, I tell them I cannot explain the what-and-why details of everything God asks us to do.

I could never have explained to Eve in the Garden of Eden why eating the forbidden fruit was such a bad idea—everything in the world being cursed to break down, people suffering and dying, man no longer having direct access to God. Those are some unbelievable consequences of biting into a single piece of fruit! In Genesis 3, Eve goes through a series of thoughts about why eating the fruit should be okay. For example, the fruit looked attractive and tasty, her body had to get nourishment from somewhere, and if it was true that eating it would allow her to gain a little wisdom, that seemed okay too. The only answer I could have given to Eve in that garden would have been, "But God said don't do it because the bad stuff that we don't understand will outweigh all the good stuff that we think we will get from living that way."

Likewise, when someone tells me they want to start using drugs or having sex outside of a one-man, one-woman marriage, I do not feel as though I have to explain exactly how their life will be worse off in the long run in human terms. I simply tell them that the Bible speaks against those actions, and that the Bible has always been correct. Of course, I can also tell them that I deeply believe following the rules that God has provided will work out best for them (and everyone else) as well, even if I can't tell them exactly how at the moment.

I stress that humans do not and cannot see all that God sees and knows. Our entire lives are defined by making decisions where every earthly example and human logic tells us to go in one direction—and the only reason we would choose a different path is because something written in a holy book thousands of years ago tells us to choose that different path. When Bible-believing Christians speak of repentance, it includes the idea that we must seek to please God with our lives and not be offensive to Him, regardless of what we think or our fellow human beings think about it. And when we use the term "faith," it includes the idea that we believe (by faith in the words of God) that following His rules—even when people do not understand or get upset about it—will make things better for all involved in the end.

10. *The origin and source of the evil and wrongdoings we commit flows from inside each one of us—and we should own up to any bad actions, rather than blame them on our environment or circumstances.* Though external forces may facilitate or exacerbate our sinful behavior, the ultimate root cause of the things we do wrong comes from our own hearts. It seems a natural, almost kneejerk reflex, when someone does something unseemly, to try and figure out what factor in their background or which environmental circumstance motivated them to behave so inappropriately. The Bible, however, teaches us that our own hearts, desires, and motives take the grand prize in this contest.

- This is an evil in all that is done under the sun, that the same event happens to all. Also, the hearts of the children of man are full of evil, and madness is in their hearts while they live, and after that they go to the dead (Eccl. 9:3).

- The heart is deceitful above all things, and desperately sick; who can understand it? (Jer. 17:9).

- And he said, "What comes out of a person is what defiles him. For from within, out of the heart of man, come evil thoughts, sexual immorality, theft, murder, adultery, coveting, wickedness, deceit, sensuality, envy, slander, pride, foolishness. All these evil things come from within, and they defile a person" (Mark 7:20–23).

- But each person is tempted when he is lured and enticed by his own desire. Then desire when it has conceived gives birth to sin, and sin when it is fully grown brings forth death (James 1:14–15).

11. *Humans are not perfect and humans cannot be made perfect while living on this earth.* It is not a matter of putting people in the right environment or giving everyone the proper training or incentives; though both can improve certain people, they absolutely will not perfect

anybody. Jesus told a parable to make sure that we understand there will be bad people who cannot and will not be transformed on this earth (Matt. 13:24–30), and the Bible clearly puts forth the idea that humans have a bent toward sin and are both incomplete and imperfect without being attached to God. Even to many non-Christians, the idea that people cannot be improved anywhere close to the point of perfection sounds like common sense, but a quick survey of history and the thoughts of a number of philosophers, politicians, and economists shows that many of the leaders of yesterday and today do believe that humans have an unlimited capacity to be improved and to become seemingly perfect. Each of these philosophies of unlimited human potential all seem to believe that it just takes the right set of conditions (devised and put into place by just the right set of leaders, of course).

Probably the best-known example of this is the writings of the father of communism, Karl Marx. Marx believed that as humans progressed into the system he described in his writings, the flaws which existed in them would slowly disappear—since these flaws were caused by the political, economic, and social institutions around them and not by their own flawed character. Of course, not all people who hold that humans have a nearly perfectible natural character are communist but they all hold a belief that is unbiblical, and all try to change the political, economic, and social institutions of the world in order to implement their philosophies. For an excellent book which discusses this theme from the political and economic rather than religious perspective, read Thomas Sowell's *A Conflict of Visions*.

Evangelical Christians simply cannot hold to this theory of good humans who have been corrupted by the things around us, because the Bible tells us that it is not so. Humans are flawed, and everything from the grace through which God provided for our salvation to the way we design our government and economic institutions needs to acknowledge human limitations.

I provide a few Bible verses below, but this topic is best defined by the opening and closing narratives of the Bible. One point we are to take from the opening—the historical narrative of Adam and Eve in the Garden of Eden—is that it was not their childhood, the environment they lived in, how other people treated them, or physical hardship that made them do something wrong. It was just the nature of being human. They had nothing to blame but human character. The closing narrative of human activity on this earth is depicted at the end of the Bible, in chapter 20 of the book of Revelation. This narrative is included in a prophecy describing the future end of this earth before God destroys it and (re-)creates a new heaven and new earth. The verses here tell us that Jesus will rule the earth with perfect justice, while Satan is held in check for a period of time. But once Jesus pulls back His reign and Satan is allowed to pressure people again, there are mass numbers of people who will choose to do wrong. Even after living with perfect Jesus under perfect justice for an extended period of time (paradise on earth, much like the Garden of Eden), humans are still bad, imperfect creatures.

Whether you take this story as literal or symbolic, one thing it is meant to teach is that everything that is wrong with human beings simply cannot and will not be fixed on this earth. To assume that humans have an unflawed character waiting to be nurtured and exercised under the crafty philosophies of brilliant men is frankly as ridiculous from a historical experience point of view as it is from the teachings of the Bible. All the major attempts to do this throughout history and across countries have failed—communism, socialism, involuntarily "reforming" criminals, etc. Any idea or program that wants to help people automatically has a Christian's attention. But any program based on removing flawed obstacles so that unflawed humans can shine through should scare those with a biblical worldview.

- . . . for all have sinned and fall short of the glory of God (Rom. 3:23).

The Bible does not say that we are not capable of *wanting* to be great, loving, honest humans—just that we cannot quite attain it, even when we want it very badly.

- For I do not understand my own actions. For I do not do what I want, but I do the very thing I hate (Rom. 7:15).

12. Especially given point 11 above, we understand that *no single human is going to be correct about everything all the time.* Whether we are speaking about some highly educated, experienced individual, or a group of "experts," mistakes will be made. And we can never really be sure which of our decisions are the incorrect ones. This is not always a pleasant way to view human nature, but the Bible says it is the correct view, and my experience also says that it is the correct view.

One interesting feature of all types of people is that we will form an opinion on a topic without having studied the various ideas and without seeking out any evidence to prove our initial stand correct. When I was in college, I taught an undergraduate economics study group as part of my graduate assistantship. To start each semester, I would have students take a stand on a couple of economic issues which were in the news at the time. I intentionally picked one issue where I knew I could present facts that would oppose the traditional conservative (or Republican) point of view, and another where I knew the facts opposed the traditional liberal (or Democrat) point of view. Ninety percent of the students would take very strong stands on both issues, and then refuse to modify their views even when I presented the facts which showed that both the "natural" conservatives and the "natural" liberals had each been wrong on one of the topics. It was actually a little disturbing to me as a teacher. My point in the exercise was to demonstrate to this mostly freshman class of students that our gut reactions on things will not always be correct. I wanted to teach them the importance of learning to think analytically (or like an economist). Instead, my first few classes of students taught me that the smarter an individual was, the *less* likely they were to acknowledge the facts were against them—and the more likely they were to use their superior intelligence to slant the facts to try to support their view or twist them into saying nothing at all.

There are a number of topics I could list here that would cause most of those reading to immediately form an opinion, even if you have not thought about or studied the topic before. For example, should children be physically spanked? If crime is a problem, should longer sentences be implemented for criminals, should more rehabilitation be provided to criminals, and/or should more cops be put on the street? If there is an overpopulation of deer in a certain residential or park area, should the problem be left alone, should the animals be trapped and relocated to another state, or should a hunt be held and some of the local population killed off?

As a side note, I should mention that my intention coming out of graduate school was to be a professor in economics, but I soon realized that the warlike energy college professors use to defend their inborn beliefs was much greater and much more dangerous than that used by my freshmen students. If most of us make decisions from the gut—decisions which support how we want the world to work, or which validate the good things we want to believe about ourselves and our friends, and the bad things we just have to believe about our enemies and are unwilling in the face of pretty solid evidence to change our minds—it helps us to understand why God calls us to trust in His ways and to be careful in having too much faith in ourselves. But understanding this human behavior also has major implications for the type of political and economic systems which will prove to be the best over time.

- There is a way that seems right to a man, but its end is the way to death (Prov. 14:12).

- There is a way that seems right to a man, but its end is the way to death (Prov. 16:25). (This must be an important lesson for us to learn, since God wrote it down for us twice in the space of just a few chapters of Proverbs—also called the book of wisdom.)

- The way of a fool is right in his own eyes, but a wise man listens to advice (Prov. 12:15).

13. *We view sin as (unsuccessful) attempts to fill in gaps left by an incomplete relationship with Christ and as (ineffective) ways to cope with the challenges we all face in an imperfect world.* We all have the need to feel loved and accepted, to feel as though we have a purpose in the world and that our lives have value and significance—and we also all have fears and anxieties. Each of these main pillars of our emotional and spiritual health are to come from a growing knowledge of and relationship with Jesus Christ. The emotional and spiritual rules Jesus provides us (even when we do not understand exactly how they benefit us) are provided by a loving God *because* they benefit us.

Why does God want to benefit us? Because it magnifies His greatness (glorifies Him) by showing His absolute mercy and love. He provides for us when we do not even know what we need, and could not provide it for ourselves even if we did understand what we needed. Every human ever born has struggled to cope with some aspect of reality. Perhaps we never learned how to overcome our own anger or fears without lashing out. Maybe we have an unrealistic need to be respected or feared. Maybe we have an unrealistic understanding of what the world owes us or of what we are entitled to, compared to other people. Some feel so overwhelmed when their environment becomes unstable they literally do not feel as though life can continue, and so they seek some type of unhealthy (sinful) relief. Because of these things, humans will seek to soothe themselves with artificial substances, to find control and power (or significance and acceptance) in sex or wealth. Many people resort to controlling others through dominance or manipulation, to release pent-up feelings of frustration or inadequacy.

Our view of sin is that using things such as drugs, sex, or anger or control to relieve the difficulties of life tends to spiral out of control on the person over time. More drugs, more money, or more power are seldom seen as a cure in and of themselves. For example, most politicians (both Republican and Democrat) seek elective office because they feel they can serve the public in some way. Some seek and achieve high levels of office, at least in part, because of their drive to exercise power over other people. Over time, the sinful use of power and control to regulate their inability to deal with the world as they should causes the positive attributes of their wanting to be public servants to be totally drowned out. Getting more and more power, and having more and more control, does not fix the issue of the person's difficulty in dealing with some aspect of the real world. This is why we see politicians getting mixed up in sex scandals of one form or another.

I have heard the question asked countless times: "Why would the governor of such and such a state, with all the power that they have, need to confirm their manhood with a prostitute?" The problem is that they have an unbiblical view of themselves and the world, and are reacting in a natural but sinful way to cope with the difficulties their self-view is creating. But they are not curing the disease—only soothing it for a very short while.

Sin is not about God's rules being too strict (the devil's ultimate lie), but about humans using pain-killers over and over to solve a problem in life—when the real solution was to have surgery to remove the source of the pain once and for all. Every human needs some Christian therapy. We all need to understand where we struggle to deal with reality, and what sinful behaviors we develop to address those issues. Arguing that we are perfectly adapted, or that God would not have the answers even if we were ill-adapted, is the foundation of rejecting Jesus as Lord.

Christians view all sin as we would view a serious drug addiction. It is easy to look at people whose lives have lost hope because of drugs, but we understand that everyone's life is exactly like that, though our drug of choice might be money, fame, power, or manipulation. There is nothing inherently wrong with money, fame, or power, just as there is nothing inherently wrong with taking morphine after major surgery. But when someone has trouble, let's say, with how they are being treated by the people in their lives, they may turn to drugs or alcohol to "soothe the pain" and escape reality for a bit. It does not matter if the people around you really are mistreating you, or if they are treating you in a very respectable way and your expectations are just out of whack and you freak out when you can't get your way. Taking drugs or drinking, to avoid the problem by trying to heal yourself, will fail in both instances. In fact, Jesus says that we certainly should not expect to always get our way, and that we will not always be treated fairly either. He says that it is how we choose to deal with being rejected or treated in an ill manner that matters. When some individuals become addicted to drugs or alcohol, they refuse to admit that their heavy use is a problem. Others will admit that their use has grown to be an issue, but still will not come to terms with the fact that the real issue is a sin against a holy God, and that it stems from some inner character flaw instead of being someone else's fault. When Christians come to understand that we all have inner character flaws and that God wants us to be honest about them and seek to overcome them, it makes this step much easier.

Fortunately, though, some addicts admit the addiction is a problem and seek to fix the issues within them that drove the problem to begin with. Of course, as all Christians are painfully aware, repenting and healing is more of a process than a single step. At some point in life, there will be a setback, and even though you know the drugs did not work out before, there is tremendous temptation to fall back into that old habit. As I have said, drugs are not the solution that everyone chooses, but the pattern of why we sin and how we deal with it is the same for drug addicts as it is for other sinners.

God asks each person to admit that the things He says are wrong are in fact wrong, and then to try and uncover their own motivations for these sins. Then we are told to seek God and His ways of adjusting our lives to overcome our inner, sinful motivations. Christians are told to show mercy in this respect, and two reasons are given. First, God has shown us mercy and forgiven us, and we should do the same for others. Second, we all sin because of personal flaws, and we have all ignored some aspect of our relationship with God. At a base level, the addicts and thieves are no different from the preachers and the missionaries. If a person refuses to admit that the sins they commit are sins, though, or they refuse to acknowledge that those sins are nobody's fault but their own, then there is nothing to which mercy can be applied.

The Bible does not tell us to excuse the behavior of an alcoholic or tell them it is okay because their dad was a drunk, too. That is not biblical mercy. The Bible tells us that we should tell the person that we are concerned about their drinking because it dishonors God and therefore must be harmful to them in some way, and that we have had issues in our lives as well, so we understand their struggle. If the person chooses to accept responsibility and work through the incredibly difficult process of recovery, then the Bible demands that we show mercy by being patient with the person, supporting them through the process, and fully forgiving and restoring them in our lives. God wants us to honor Him by intentionally choosing to follow His guidelines with the faith that they are best for us (even when we do not understand why), and He wants us to seek the entire purpose, meaning, and direction in our lives from Him.

- The thief comes only to steal and kill and destroy. I came that they may have life and have it abundantly (John 10:10).

- And he said, "What comes out of a person is what defiles him. For from within, out of the heart of man, come evil thoughts, sexual immorality, theft, murder, adultery, coveting, wickedness, deceit, sensuality, envy, slander, pride, foolishness. All these evil things come from within, and they defile a person" (Mark 7:20–23).

14. *Sin has cursed the world, and the curses of sin (sickness, pain, poverty, death, etc.) will not/cannot be eliminated on this current earth.* God did not originally create a world cursed with pain, suffering, and death. The appropriate concern is not "Why did God create a world where people suffer?" but "Look what man has done to God's

perfect creation; I wish we had all chosen His ways and not cursed ourselves." All Christians wait for the day when God fixes the mess that we should never have made in the first place. The main reason that we should hate sin and try and set our mind against sinning is because it dishonors our holy God and Creator. But another reason that we should hate sin is because it harms God's creation, including other people. All of this sin could be used as an excuse for not doing anything to help out those in need, but the Bible is full of commands from God (in both the Old Testament and New Testament) that we must make the world a better place to live in, by helping those who cannot help themselves and by letting the light of Christ shine through us in our good deeds. In a number of different passages in the gospel accounts of the life of Jesus, the authors tell us that while Jesus was going between one important task for God and another, He would see someone suffering and "having compassion on them," He would stop and help them out.

Christians have ministries to help tutor kids who struggle with reading, provide hospitals for the sick, foster homes for the abandoned, comfort for the imprisoned, food banks for the hungry, rehabilitation for the elderly, and hospice care for the dying. We do all these things because Jesus tells us that in doing them, glory will be brought to God the Father. The key is that although Christians must help alleviate suffering and defend those who are treated unjustly by society (Matt. 25:31–46), we must not forget that we will never entirely eliminate poverty, sickness, and injustice from the earth. Only God will do that, when Christ comes back. Just because a patient's life cannot be saved does not mean that a medical professional should not comfort them and manage their pain as they die. And just because we cannot end world poverty or political or criminal injustice does not mean that Christians should not make every effort to do our part. But we must not get caught up in thinking that we will ultimately and finally cure the curses of this earth, or else our initiatives will be skewed in the wrong directions, and the harm of frustration and finger pointing will overrule any good that we do.

- And to Adam he said, "Because you have listened to the voice of your wife and have eaten of the tree of which I commanded you, 'You shall not eat of it,' cursed is the ground because of you; in pain you shall eat of it all the days of your life; thorns and thistles it shall bring forth for you; and you shall eat the plants of the field. By the sweat of your face you shall eat bread, till you return to the ground, for out of it you were taken; for you are dust, and to dust you shall return" (Gen. 3:17–19).

- For you always have the poor with you, but you do not always have me (John 12:8).

- For we know that the whole creation has been groaning together in the pains of childbirth until now. And not only the creation, but we ourselves, who have the firstfruits of the Spirit, groan inwardly as we wait eagerly for adoption as sons, the redemption of our bodies (Rom. 8:22–23).

- Religion that is pure and undefiled before God, the Father, is this: to visit orphans and widows in their affliction, and to keep oneself unstained from the world. (James 1:27).

- No longer will there be anything accursed, but the throne of God and of the Lamb will be in it, and his servants will worship him (Rev. 22:3).

- Honor widows who are truly widows. But if a widow has children or grandchildren, let them first learn to show godliness to their own household and to make some return to their parents, for this is pleasing in the sight of God. She who is truly a widow, left all alone, has set her hope on God and continues in supplications and prayers night and day (1 Tim. 5:3–5).

15. *Though humans have a natural tendency to positively identify with those who are like us, and to suspect and distrust those who are not, an important principle which is to guide our life is that we are to be for God*

rather than against anything else—and that we are to take responsibility for ourselves rather than blaming our enemies. The simplest lesson we are to take from this is that we are not to be bigots. Psychologists have repeatedly validated the notion that humans tend to distrust those who are different from us. The classic academic work on the subject is Gordon Allport's *The Nature of Prejudice.*

There are verses in the Old and New Testament which explicitly forbid us from being bigots (for example, Leviticus 19:33–34, and the story of the Good Samaritan in Luke 10:25–37—the meaning of which is not that we should do nice deeds for one another, but to teach us not to be racist). The bigotry of which we must be careful, though, is not just confined to race or ethnicity. Humans find all manner of differences to key off of in the modern world. Those in academics (faculty and students) demonize those in the business world; those who play lacrosse make fun of those who play basketball or soccer, and on and on it goes. The Bible teaches us to look for and cultivate the commonalities between us, rather than focus on the differences.

There is a related problem to this issue of liking those similar to us, and of having a tendency to take a stand against those with whom we differ, that must be discussed as well: We cannot allow others to use this negative trait in our human nature to manipulate us by turning us toward a common enemy. In some of His earliest and most important teachings, Jesus tells us that we will know a good leader from a bad leader by the fruit that is yielded in their lives, by the outcome of their own personal actions—not by what they say, or by what we have in common with them.

These two areas are related to each other in the Bible. For Christians, it is extremely important that we serve Jesus and are loyal to Him, not to some church organization or some smooth-talking leader or manmade movement. We all know how easy it is for leaders to get people to focus on a common enemy as a justification for having power. The enemy does not even have to be real. The communist dictators in North Korea have ruled over their people for decades by drilling in their heads that South Korea, America, or Japan are going to invade any minute. The people do not like and have nothing in common with the dictators, but live much of their lives based around this made-up common enemy.

Of course, this is done in a subtler fashion in American politics all the time. It is amazing how many politicians will make campaign speeches or bring bills up to be passed as laws in Congress and only mention their political enemies, with nothing said about the constituents whom the new law is supposed to actually help. Churches can fall prey to this just as easily as any other group or organization. Therefore, we remind ourselves constantly that Jesus is King, and take our actions based on serving and glorifying the King rather than on defeating or seeking revenge against an enemy. It is God's job to deal with and defeat the enemy, not ours.

When leaders or organizations seek power and control, they will often use the common-enemy theme to bond people together, and we can easily be drawn to support others who say all the right things and have qualities that we admire in a person. But Jesus tells us that if someone is not for God, we should not follow them; and if the consequences of someone's life are harmful, then we should cease to follow them as well.

Again, we can pick on politicians for our examples. When a famous politician of either party produces bad (often illegal) fruit in their lives, people who identify with the same party always seem to find some excuse for that person's behavior (even when they were horrified when someone of the other party did something similar before). This happens with both Republicans and Democrats. The Bible would teach us, however, that we cannot become so engrossed with another person that we refuse to see their flaws, and that we should never ignore the flaws we see in someone simply because we share a common enemy with that person. In the church, this can happen when Christians start to feel as though the world is against us. TV shows, judges, and Hollywood all seem opposed to us, so we have to be careful not to fall into the common-enemy trap.

There is another, perhaps subtler, issue related to the common-enemy problem. I mentioned in point 10, relative to the causes of our sins, that we must be willing to admit that our missteps are our fault. When we are under the influence (our own, or that of a charismatic leader) of the "they're not like me" or common-enemy hex, it becomes much too easy to shirk personal responsibility for our losses and flaws—and instead to cast blame on those who are different from us, assuming this difference naturally makes them opposed to us. Taking responsibility for ourselves and our actions first and foremost is a key element of the biblical worldview.

- For we do not wrestle against flesh and blood (Eph. 6:12).

- Beware of false prophets, who come to you in sheep's clothing but inwardly are ravenous wolves. You will recognize them by their fruits. Are grapes gathered from thornbushes, or figs from thistles? (Matt. 7:15–16).

16. *In the ways that are important to God, all people are equal.* Of course, some people are taller or more athletic, or have the inborn ability to make friends or make money easily. God granted only to women the ability to carry and give birth to children. All people are not identical in every conceivable way but we are all equal in terms of being made in God's image, and we all have equal worth in the eyes of God and the church. Those who are smarter, richer, or better-looking are not superior. Those born into upper-class families are not superior.

One of the greatest human character flaws is our need to identify another class of people as being inferior to us. It is fine for someone in Mexico to be proud of their country, just as it is fine for Americans to be proud of our country. But it is wrong to feel as though we are somehow "superior" to those in other countries (whether it is an ally such as Mexico, or the citizens of a country which has declared itself our enemy such as North Korea). Our being created equal by God does not guarantee that we will all achieve—or all have the God-given right to achieve—equality in every area of life. Some will excel in sports and others will not. Some will have both parents in their lives until they are grown, while others may lose a parent to death or divorce. Some will achieve their economic goals early, and some will never fully achieve them. Some will have both a lasting and happy marriage; some will have neither.

One of the measures of equality that God is concerned about is written about by James the brother of Jesus, in his letter in the New Testament portion of the Bible. James said that if we see a poor, unknown person and a rich, famous person come into our church, we should not show favoritism to the celebrity (James 2:1–7). Of course, this rule also applies outside of the pews in a sanctuary. If you saw a person who appeared to have no standing in the community struggling to carry something across the street in your hometown, would you provide him or her the same assistance you would if it were your boss, or your favorite sports star or musician?

It is natural for many of us to just automatically assume that different people have different worth. Again, it is not unbiblical to say that only the person who can pass a medical exam can be a doctor and perform operations. Rules such as this will distinguish certain professional classes in society, and that is more than acceptable. The Bible clearly demonstrates that some people are better designed to be generals, and others regular soldiers.

But if people from two very different professional or social classes were in trouble, would you be equally likely to help each one? If people from two different professional or social classes were to become entangled in some type of legal trouble, would you be equally likely to condemn each one? Would you rather spend time with a celebrity, or with a volunteer at a local school? Related to this is the idea Jesus taught that leaders are to be the biggest servants of all, not those who wield the most power and accrue the most privilege.

- My brothers, show no partiality as you hold the faith in our Lord Jesus Christ, the Lord of glory. For if a man wearing a gold ring and fine clothing comes into your assembly, and a poor man in shabby clothing also comes in, and if you pay attention to the one who wears the fine clothing and say, "You sit here in a good place," while you say to the poor man, "You stand over there," or, "Sit down at my feet," have you not then made distinctions among yourselves and become judges with evil thoughts? (James 2:1–4)

• And Jesus called them to him and said to them, "You know that those who are considered rulers of the Gentiles lord it over them, and their great ones exercise authority over them. But it shall not be so among you. But whoever would be great among you must be your servant, and whoever would be first among you must be slave of all. For even the Son of Man came not to be served but to serve, and to give his life as a ransom for many" (Mark 10:42–45).

17. *Money is not the only thing that matters; it is not even close to being the most important thing that matters.* On the surface this sounds obvious to most people, but when we look at our actions, we sometimes see that they suggest we really *do* believe money is the most important thing. Some act as if it is the *only* important thing. Survey after survey after survey has shown that up to a point, money does increase happiness, because it is hard to be perfectly content if you are hungry, sick, or without safe shelter or transportation. But at the point where we are living a safe life and begin to view money in terms of how much of it we could lose or how much more we need to compare to other people, the happiness factor stops increasing and can actually go down.

I have only known a few people who have won any money at all while gambling or playing the lottery (and these were not million-dollar winners) but I know that their life did not improve with their new fortunes. And I have literally read dozens of accounts in local newspapers where someone hits a million-plus-dollar lottery, and a few years later are divorced and bankrupt. There are many things that I would wish for myself and my family (great health, strong emotional relationships, success in our religious, academic, and professional endeavors, etc.), but winning the lottery or coming into millions of dollars through an inheritance would absolutely not be one of them. Money is great because it allows me to exchange the work that I do for the products and services that other people work to create, and it is a convenient way to save up for a rainy day. But money is just not that important. I do not want my life revolving around money. I do not want to measure my or your worth with money. It is useful and has its purpose, but it just is not all that important.

- You cannot serve God and money (Matt. 6:24).

- For the love of money is a root of all kinds of evils. It is through this craving that some have wandered away from the faith and pierced themselves with many pangs (1 Tim. 6:10).

18. *God has set eternity in man's heart. He gives us a desire to connect with Him and to be part of something bigger than ourselves—something with a lasting impact.* This does not just mean we are created with a desire to leave a legacy through earthly accomplishments. God has created a longing in us to be more united with Him, and to be a part of something that is bigger and longer-lasting than just our own personal satisfaction. In his book *Vertical Church*, James MacDonald writes about our need to connect with God, and to search for meaning and fulfillment vertically through God instead of horizontally through man and earthly endeavors. All humans feel the need to be part of something bigger than ourselves, even something that will outlast us on the earth. Some want to live on through their children; others might make large donations and have buildings built in their name which will survive long after they have died. Some work to save the environment, or something else of particular interest to them.

But the Bible tells us that ultimately we have to be connected to God and work in His earthly kingdom, in order to truly satisfy this need for eternal significance that God has placed in our hearts. It is fine to work on buildings, or to mentor young kids, but unless there is a God-connected, God-glorifying purpose, we will continue to search for this ultimate significance all our lives.

There are many types of behaviors which can overtake us and consume our lives, as we struggle to deal with the difficulties of reality and our own unique place in a harsh world. One of the items that can overtake us is this internal drive of wanting to make a lasting impression with our lives. If we do not understand that this basic drive is within us and that God designed us to satisfy it, the search for our lasting impact can make us very cynical (as we will see in later chapters), and even haunt our lives and destroy us from the inside out. Understanding what feelings and motivations God has given us, and seeking to fulfill them as He instructs us, is one of the best ways to guarantee an inner peace and contentment that too few people ever truly know.

- He has made everything beautiful in its time. Also, he has put eternity into man's heart, yet so that he cannot find out what God has done from the beginning to the end (Eccl. 3:11).

19. *People have a need to feel good about themselves in a moral, righteous sense.* There are many characteristics which people seem to desire universally: being independent and responsible, being good at something, being respected by others, being needed by others. Most people also want others to understand and appreciate their moral goodness as well. Though different people place a different priority level on being moral, its importance does register with most. And for some, it is a critical element in how they view themselves, and it becomes very important in how they define their life and identity. However, it is very easy for this to slip into a need to show our morality to others, or to feel that we are morally superior to others.

One of the ways that we know we are slipping away from truly desiring to be a good person and into the pit of moral superiority is described by Jesus in His ministry over and over while He was on earth. He says that a good tree is known by its good fruit and a bad tree by its bad fruit (Luke 6:44). By this He means that what we say and how we draw comparisons between ourselves and others is irrelevant, because what matters is what comes from our activities—not who commends us for them or what "credit" we get for the activity, not how they make us feel and not how they stack up to what others have done, but what benefit accrues to others.

Jesus challenged the leaders of His day, stating that in their desire to appear to others that they were moral, and in their need to convince themselves that they were morally superior to others, they were asking others to bear burdens they were not willing to tolerate themselves—and that their actions, and the results of their actions, were incredibly hypocritical (Matt. 23:2–7). Christ challenged these leaders to see that their focus had shifted at some point toward trying to persuade themselves they were good people, and in caring more about how they *appeared* to others, and away from how "good" they truly were on the inside.

20. *We can only get true righteousness and good moral standing through Jesus Christ.* The Bible teaches us that, though we should endeavor to live lives of integrity and character, we cannot attain our own moral righteousness through anything we do, nor from any religious rules we follow. This is plain in Old Testament as well as New Testament verses.

- Truly no man can ransom another, or give to God the price of his life, for the ransom of their life is costly and can never suffice, that he should live on forever and never see the pit (Ps. 49:7–9).

- The righteousness of God through faith in Jesus Christ for all who believe. For there is no distinction: for all have sinned and fall short of the glory of God, and are justified by his grace as a gift, through the redemption that is in Christ Jesus (Rom. 3:22–24).

- Brothers, my heart's desire and prayer to God for them is that they may be saved. For I bear them witness that they have a zeal for God, but not according to knowledge. For, being ignorant of the righteousness of God, and seeking to establish their own, they did not submit to God's righteousness (Rom. 10:1–3).

- For by grace you have been saved through faith. And this is not your own doing; it is the gift of God, not a result of works, so that no one may boast (Eph. 2:8–9).

21. *God ordained three main institutions to provide structure to human life—the family, the government, and the church.* As they are established and described in Scripture, it is clear that the three are designed to complement one another, and even overlap a bit. However, they are not interchangeable; each was designed with, and should be limited to, its specific purpose.

22. *The main functions of the family are for men and women to be life-long "helpmates" in serving God and to produce and raise godly children.* Simply put, husbands and wives are to complement each other, using their joint life together to glorify God. Husbands and wives are to not only be the source of new babies in the world, but to be the primary providers for their children's physical and emotional wellbeing, and the main influence over their spiritual lives as well. Some (perhaps most famously, Hillary Clinton) have said they believe that it "takes a village to raise a child," apparently meaning that individual mom and dads can't be trusted to raise their children without the direction of all the brilliant people in the government. But the Bible says that is not true—it takes a family to raise a child.

- Then the LORD God said, "It is not good that the man should be alone; I will make him a helper fit for him" (Gen. 2:18).

- Therefore a man shall leave his father and his mother and hold fast to his wife, and they shall become one flesh (Gen. 2:24).

- So God created man in his own image, in the image of God he created him; male and female he created them. And God blessed them. And God said to them, "Be fruitful and multiply" (Gen. 1: 27–28a).

- Only take care, and keep your soul diligently, lest you forget the things that your eyes have seen, and lest they depart from your heart all the days of your life. Make them known to your children and your children's children (Deut. 4:9).

- You shall love the LORD your God with all your heart and with all your soul and with all your might. And these words that I command you today shall be on your heart. You shall teach them diligently to your children, and shall talk of them when you sit in your house, and when you walk by the way, and when you lie down, and when you rise (Deut. 6:5–7).

- You shall therefore lay up these words of mine in your heart and in your soul, and you shall bind them as a sign on your hand, and they shall be as frontlets between your eyes. You shall teach them to your children, talking of them when you are sitting in your house, and when you are walking by the way, and when you lie down, and when you rise (Deut. 11:18–19).

23. *The main function of governments and the laws they pass is to protect citizens from the harm of others.* The Bible teaches that a government's main role is to protect its citizens from being harmed by other citizens—to restrain the evil nature of human beings (Rom. 13:1–7). The Bible says that people will cause harm to each other and that crimes should be punished (Prov. 17: 15; 18:5; 24:23–25). Jesus also taught us that we should support the government (Matt. 22:15–22) unless the government is directly and intentionally dishonoring God (Acts 5:27–32), and that we are not to rely on the government to enforce everything that we consider a sin.

There is an interesting story in John 8:1–11, where Jesus helps to make this last point for us. At the time that Christ lived in Israel, the legal authority belonged to the Roman government. As such, only Rome could enforce legal statutes, especially those relating to capital punishment. Some religious leaders brought a woman who was caught in the act of adultery to Jesus, and asked Him to try and enforce an old rule that had applied when the Jewish people had their own theocracy (religious-based government). Jesus acted as a religious leader, reminding the woman that what she had done was sinful in the eyes of God and encouraging her to not sin anymore, but refused to act as a law enforcement officer or judge.

Of course, people will often try to use what is in the Bible to determine what the country's laws should be. For example, President

Obama referenced his Christian faith and the demands of Scripture as a reason for some of his policies at a National Prayer Breakfast in February 2012. But having a biblical worldview does not mean every sin should be against the law, or that every biblical command should be required by law. It is sinful to disobey your parents, to cuss, or to be drunk in your own home, but it is unrealistic to make those behaviors against the law. Jesus taught us that we should pray continuously and not give up, but that is not something the government should attempt to legally encode. A government's primary responsibility is to restrain the harm of one person or group against another—not to create a "perfect" world, nor to make every biblical sin punishable by law.

I will close out this point by mentioning what political scientists call "public goods." These are services that are difficult for regular businesses in the private sector to provide, either because of the scale required or because of the difficulty in charging for the product in the marketplace. A couple of common examples of public goods are a military and a police force. Of course, those fit well with our Romans 13 definition of the role of government. There are, however, some services—flood control being a classic case—which are pure examples of public goods as well. Though the main function of government, as described in the Bible, is to restrain the evil of the strong against the weak, having the government provide other public goods such as flood control is not antibiblical at all.

24. *When our desire to be involved in something bigger than ourselves (number 18) is coupled with our need to feel and appear morally good to others (number 19), humans can become self-righteous and hypocritical. And when in this state of mind (given number 15), we will tend to become defensive, closing ranks with those who agree and taking extremely negative views of those who disagree with us.* This is an issue which Jesus sternly and directly chastised the leaders of His day about, and His rebukes of them serve as a warning for us today. Serious Bible-believing Christians are ever-vigilant on this issue, many having accountability partners to keep them honest on this front.

In His commentary on the current political, social, and religious trends of His day, Jesus seemed most agitated by (and reserved most of His criticism for) the self-righteous crowd. When reading the Bible, some people are amazed at how lightly Jesus seems to scold sinners (including the likes of thieves and prostitutes), yet how aggressive He is in condemning the self-righteous. In defense of themselves, these individuals knew they had a desire to be a part of something bigger than their own life. They were trying to be good people and leave a positive mark on the world. In the beginning their motives seemed reasonable, if not admirable. So why all the lectures from Jesus?

As you read through His comments, it is easy to build an understanding of Jesus' issue here. As stated in point 20 above, none of us are really righteous and holy in and of ourselves. But for many of us (number 19), that is a critical point of both how we want to be able to view ourselves and how we want (or demand) that others view us as well. The main issue Jesus had with this is that it leads to a series of interconnected cycles which violate multiple points of the biblical worldview. If the causes to which we attach ourselves are larger than ourselves in scope (number 18), it exacerbates these potentially negative outcomes.

If I desperately want a self-identity or public perception as a good moral person—either because I want to leave a positive legacy, or because I have guilty feelings about my actions in another area of my life—I may find it easier to puff up my own contributions and viciously attack those who won't acknowledge my contributions than to actually do the extremely hard (and usually unrecognized) day-to-day work of making the world a better place. In addition to this, Jesus noted over and over that when our self-identity or how we are viewed by others begins to dominate over the original desire to be a good person involved in issues bigger than ourselves, we are likely to become hypocrites.

As an example: If I speak about helping out the poor in my area, society will usually give me credit for being a decent person. If

I become more interested in that approval than in actually helping the poor improve their lot (which can be time-consuming, thankless work), it will be easier to ratchet up my speech about helping the poor rather than to actually invest more time and sweat into directly helping them. Obviously, it will not take long before my words (both those proclaiming my deeds and intentions, and those challenging others to step up) exceed both my willingness and ability to work against local poverty. As this process continues, and the gap widens between what I claim should be done for the poor compared to the actual results of what I am doing, I will focus more and more on talking rather than doing—and the talk will become increasingly focused on what others are *not* doing. Jesus reprimanded people in His day for that:

- Woe to you, scribes and Pharisees, hypocrites! For you clean the outside of the cup and the plate, but inside they are full of greed and self-indulgence. You blind Pharisee! First clean the inside of the cup and the plate, that the outside also may be clean. Woe to you, scribes and Pharisees, hypocrites! For you are like whitewashed tombs, which outwardly appear beautiful, but within are full of dead people's bones and all uncleanness. So you also outwardly appear righteous to others, but within you are full of hypocrisy and lawlessness (Matt. 23:25–28).

In today's world, we all make fun of politicians and celebrities for banging the drums of their favorite causes while at best doing nothing to further the cause, and more often than not hypocritically living in violation of the very things they claim are so worthy—for example, entertainers who decry all those who aren't environmentally friendly enough to meet their standards, but fly around in private jets between their multiple mansions with heated pools (burning more fossil fuels than I ever dreamed of in the process); politicians who send their kids to private schools while voting down public vouchers which would allow those who are less affluent to send their children to private schools; or billionaires who pay accountants to minimize their tax burden, while scolding others that they should all be paying more taxes.

Of course, if it is the public recognition I am after (in lieu of or in addition to the self-identity dimension) then the "righteous" deeds I aspire to must be recognized as such by the group I am interested in impressing. Unfortunately, history has proven that humans don't always pick good items to encourage one another with in this regard (partly because of what the Bible refers to as our bent toward sin, and partly because of what psychiatrists call "group think"). Then, in order to increase the feelings of elevated, relative morality that is sought, I will spur the group I belong to into becoming obsessed with criticizing other groups which do not (fully) agree with my group (number 15 above). This cycle hits its ultimate level of absurdity when one group chooses the causes they promote based on what is not promoted (or not approved of) by a group with which they have disagreed in the past.

Jesus never explicitly warned us about the dangers of those who seek to kidnap or kill us. But He warns us over and over about this self-righteous crowd, calling them false prophets (because they don't even follow what they say, and the warnings they give never materialize) and telling us to beware of them.

- Beware of false prophets, who come to you in sheep's clothing but inwardly are ravenous wolves. You will recognize them by their fruits. Are grapes gathered from thornbushes, or figs from thistles? (Matt. 7:15–16).

Our common sense tells us to beware of someone coming at us with a weapon, but it is easy to get caught up when influential people in society (religious, government or business leaders, entertainers, university professors, etc.) are making claims against my actions and demanding I change my course based on their reasoning and moral persuasion. But Jesus plainly says beware of them if they are hypocrites, or if their predictions are not coming true.

Those holding a biblical worldview react here on two fronts. First, as stated above, we have to constantly guard ourselves from becoming the hypocritical false prophets. And only second do we keep our guard up, so that we are not harmed by such people.

25. *Motives are what matter most in the Christian faith. Given how number 19 above can be twisted, we must guard against impure motives causing us to add (usually external) elements and traditions to the true religion which God has revealed to us.* As already mentioned, Jesus tells us very directly that the two greatest commandments are to love God and love other people. Love itself cannot be faked, but the outward expressions of it can. Both the Old Testament prophets and Jesus scold those of us who say or even do the appropriate things but do them for less than honorable reasons. In fact, a tidy summary of what we today call Jesus' Sermon on the Mount (Matt. 5–7) would be, "You have been told by God before to act or not act in a certain way but I am telling you that the motivations that come from your heart are more important than the acts themselves."

   In addition to only acting as though we love God or others and/ or doing things for the wrong motives, we have a tendency to get stuck in manmade habits and traditions, sometimes for the self-righteous reasons of impressing others and attempting to elevate ourselves above them spiritually, but often simply for the sake of custom and comfort. The bent toward doing or not doing various deeds to make ourselves feel or appear more morally righteous, or becoming trapped in extrabiblical processes, is the reason each individual believer and each generation of Christians must return to the Scriptures again and again as the foundation for our beliefs, our religious practices, and our very worldview.

   • And you, Solomon my son, know the God of your father and serve him with a whole heart and with a willing mind, for the LORD searches all hearts and understands every plan and thought. If you seek him, he will be found by you, but if you forsake him, he will cast you off forever (1 Chron. 28:9).

- All the ways of a man are pure in his own eyes, but the LORD weighs the spirit (Prov. 16:2).

- Every way of a man is right in his own eyes, but the LORD weighs the heart. To do righteousness and justice is more acceptable to the LORD than sacrifice (Prov. 21:2–3).

- And the Lord said: "Because this people draw near with their mouth and honor me with their lips, while their hearts are far from me, and their fear of me is a commandment taught by men, therefore, behold, I will again do wonderful things with this people, with wonder upon wonder; and the wisdom of their wise men shall perish, and the discernment of their discerning men shall be hidden" (Isa. 29:13–14).

- Blessed are the pure in heart, for they shall see God (Matt. 5:8)

- Beware of practicing your righteousness before other people in order to be seen by them, for then you will have no reward from your Father who is in heaven (Matt. 6:1).

- And the Pharisees and the scribes asked him, "Why do your disciples not walk according to the tradition of the elders, but eat with defiled hands?" And he said to them, "Well did Isaiah prophesy of you hypocrites, as it is written, 'This people honors me with their lips, but their heart is far from me; in vain do they worship me, teaching as doctrines the commandments of men.' You leave the commandment of God and hold to the tradition of men" (Mark 7:5–8).

- Beloved, although I was very eager to write to you about our common salvation, I found it necessary to write appealing to you to contend for the faith that was once for all delivered to the saints (Jude 1:3).

As a recap, here are the twenty-five elements that begin to define the biblical worldview:

1. God (through Jesus) created everything and everything was created with the purpose of glorifying God.

2. The overarching purpose, then, of our individual lives is to glorify God.

3. We glorify God by allowing our lives to be changed and through our service to others.

4. Religious texts and teachings are to be evaluated and validated on the success of their explanations and predictions.

5. The beginning of our knowledge and wisdom comes from a healthy reverence for God and the Scriptures He had written down for us.

6. God's physical creation works in a consistent, systematic way that can be discovered.

7. Building off numbers 4, 5 and 6 above, as God's earthly stewards, we are to accumulate knowledge so we can continue to subdue the earth and have dominion over it. We do this through testing theories, options, and processes, keeping the ones which can predict and explain and throwing out the ones proven to be false.

8. Though other animals are not, man is more than a physical being.

9. The requirements and instructions God provides for us to live by deal in absolute rights and wrongs and they are best for us, ultimately allowing us the most abundant life. Satan's biggest lie is that there are no absolute rights and wrongs and that God's rules are unfair and restrict our enjoying the best possible life.

10. The origin and source of the evil and wrongdoings we commit flows from inside each one of us, and we should own up to any bad actions rather than blame them on our environment or circumstances.

11. Humans are not perfect, and humans cannot be made perfect while living on this earth.

12. No single human is going to be correct about everything all the time.

13. Sins are (unsuccessful) attempts to fill in gaps left by an incomplete relationship with Christ, and (ineffective) ways to cope with the challenges we all face in an imperfect world.

14. Sin has cursed the world, and the curses of sin (sickness, pain, poverty, death, etc.) will not/cannot be eliminated on this current earth.

15. Though humans have a natural tendency to positively identify with those who are like us, and to suspect and distrust those who are not, an important principle which is to guide our life is that we are to be for God rather than against anything else. We are to take responsibility for ourselves, rather than blaming our enemies.

16. In the ways that are important to God, all people are equal.

17. Money is not the only thing that matters; it is not even close to being the most important thing that matters.

18. God has set eternity in man's heart. He gives us a desire to connect to Him and to be part of something bigger than ourselves—something with a lasting impact.

19. People have a need to feel good about themselves in a moral, righteous sense.

20. We can only get true righteousness and good moral standing through Jesus Christ.

21. God ordained three main institutions to provide structure to human life—the family, the government, and the church.

22. The main functions of the family are for men and women to be lifelong "helpmates" in serving God and to produce and raise godly children.

23. The main function of governments and the laws they pass is to protect citizens from the harm of others.

24. When our desire to be involved in something bigger than ourselves (number 18) is coupled with our need to feel and appear morally good to others (number 19), humans can become self-righteous and hypocritical. And when in this state of mind (given

number 15), we will tend to become defensive, closing ranks with those who agree and taking extremely negative views of those who disagree with us.

25. Motives are what matter most in the Christian faith. Given how number 19 above can be twisted, we must guard against impure motives causing us to add (usually external) elements and traditions to the true religion which God has revealed to us.

These twenty-five high-level principles are necessary if we are to get a clear vision of what the Bible teaches us about the nature of our world, and the nature of ourselves. But the Bible does not explicitly explain, in detail, everything we need to understand all the subjects covered in the following chapters. Instead it teaches us—through the words of Jesus in Matthew 7, and the lesson encapsulated in point 7 above—that, where applicable, we are to determine what is best or optimal, and what is not, by rejecting failed hypotheses and letting go of explanations when their predictions fail to come true.

We combine this rational approach with the twenty-five principles above to get our clear vision of how the Bible teaches us to view the world. In some cases we will lean more heavily on the twenty-five principles and in others, as will be made clear, on empirical evidence.

CHAPTER 4

The View of Politics

If those with a biblical worldview could design the ideal mix of political parties in the House of Representatives and the Senate, what would that mix be?

a. 100% Republican

b. 100% Democrat

c. a 50/50 mix of Republicans & Democrats

The answer is "c." But more on this a few paragraphs down. First let's deal with another question: In which of our country's founding documents will you find the often-repeated phrase "the separation of church and state"?

a. The Declaration of Independence

b. The Constitution of the United States

c. The Bill of Rights, attached to the Constitution

d. All of the above

e. None of the above

The answer is "e." In fact, that phrase is in no government document at all, and never has been. The phrase was written in a private letter by an individual who wrote in other places, such as his *Notes on the State of Virginia*, that he, as a white man, considered blacks to be both physically and mentally inferior to whites. Wow, nice guy. Why do so many people quote such a line today as if it were a real law written in stone, especially if it is not written anywhere official?

Probably the easiest answer to why the phrase "separation of church and state" is the single most misused statement in American politics is because it is all that those who are opposed to religion in this country have to cling to. The founding document of this country—in its first two sentences—mentions God and assigns Him the role of making the laws of nature; this is before stating directly and intentionally that all the natural rights we have as humans—rights that can't be compromised by another human because they are core to our existence—come from God our Creator. With this as the backdrop, there are actually few other straws for non-religious folks to grasp at, other than a misquoted line from some personal letter written two-hundred-plus years ago by a self-declared racist.

Let me reprint those first two sentences from America's founding document, highlighting the phrases referenced above:

> When in the Course of human events, it becomes necessary for one people to dissolve the political bands which have connected them with another, and to assume among the powers of the earth, *the separate and equal station to which the Laws of Nature and of Nature's God entitle them,* a decent respect to the opinions of mankind requires that they should declare the causes which impel them to the separation. *We hold these truths to be self-evident, that all men are created equal, that they are endowed by their Creator with certain unalienable Rights,* that among these are Life, Liberty and the pursuit of Happiness.

The conclusion of the Declaration of Independence also speaks of the representatives of the United States "appealing to the Supreme Judge of the world." The founders of this country said that it was self-evident that God created us and meant for us to have certain rights, just because we are humans made in His image. And they did this for a very important reason. If they had set up America as a separate country based on rights given to us by our political human founders, subsequent human politicians would simply have been able to change those rights. We see this happen with all types of other laws and political issues. One day a political body makes something legal or illegal; soon enough, new politicians are elected and change the law. If we have permanent rights given to us by God, however, they cannot be overturned by men. Our country is literally built on the notion of God existing, and God providing the foundation for our most basic freedoms.

I understand that some people do not believe in God, or believe but do not think it appropriate that the very notion of God should be woven into the legal founding and fabric of our republic. But that is the way the country was founded. As my parents used to say when I would complain about something that I could not change, "It is what it is." I have had conversations with people who do not think that we should have an elected body which is not based on population (such as the US Senate). Many others do not like directly electing the president, because they believe the holder of that position should be chosen from among the directly elected representatives in the House of Representatives (as some prime ministers are in other countries). If each of us scanned the Declaration of Independence and the Constitution with all its amendments, I suspect we all would find something that is not to our liking, shaking our heads and asking "What were the founding fathers thinking with that one?" It is okay to wish that God was not mentioned in our founding documents as the basis for our legal rights, but it is not okay to pretend as if that is not the case or try to legally regulate around it.

Of course, there is another statement dealing with religion in the Bill of Rights to the Constitution: "Congress shall make no law respecting an establishment of religion, or prohibiting the free exercise thereof." That simply means that the Constitution prohibited the government from establishing an official state religion and/or forbade the government from taxing its citizens and giving the money to one particular denomination. The second part of the sentence states that the government cannot pass statutes making it illegal to worship, or forbidding people from privately and publicly practicing the religion of their choice.

Most people know, but some do not, that it was the religious organizations of the day who requested this be the first Amendment in the Bill of Rights. A great portion of the people who took the incredible risk to come to America—and then fight for its freedom—came from Europe, so that they could practice their religion freely. They were fed up with their native governments taxing their money to give it to religious establishments (such as the Catholic and Anglican churches) where they did not worship and did not desire to support. They also saw how the mix of politics and religion was bad for both.

No Bible-believing Christian today would dare want the government to support a particular denomination with tax money, because we do not want the government dictating what we can and cannot do. We only want the Bible to dictate our beliefs and the actions we take within our churches. And neither evangelical Christians of yesterday, nor those of today, want a "religious government" where the leaders of some church are also by default the political leaders of the country. But we do understand that the God of the Bible was important to the founding of the country, and that without invoking God and the rights He gave us—which we cannot surrender and cannot take away from each other—our country could change for the worse on a whim. The country's founding documents set us up as a God-believing nation and that can never be changed (without completely deconstructing the United States of America and building a new nation on this land).

Government Form and Political Parties

In discussing the type of government that those with a biblical worldview prefer, we need to go back to point 23 from our previous chapter, and remind ourselves what the Bible says is the primary purpose of government: to protect us from, and bring wrath upon, those who do evil against others.

While most Christians do actively participate in elections and some even run for office, again, there is no desire by Christians to institute a "government of religion." Well, if not a religious-based theocracy, then what? Based on Bible verses such as Proverbs 18:17 and the experience provided by history, evangelical Christians strongly prefer democracy to any other type of government structure. Democracies spend their time governing the lives of their people and protecting them from harm, while other forms of government spend too much time protecting themselves and striking out against internal enemies. Humans have only truly been free to pursue the things most important to them and their families when they have lived under democratic rule. My greatest desire would be for all people to come to a saving knowledge of Jesus Christ as their Lord and Savior, to repent and turn toward God and be obedient in baptism. But while we are all living on the earth, and whether you believe in the same God as me or not, it is certainly best if we can all live with protection of our individual freedom. Democracy seems to be the only way man has devised to ensure that this will happen consistently, generation after generation.

Democracies have always done best in Christian societies but there is more to it than that. In a fascinating paper entitled "The Missionary Roots of Liberal Democracy," Robert Woodberry of the University of Texas shows that missionaries sent out to evangelize the world have helped to promote and install democracy around the globe, believing it to be the best form of government to preside over the people they had come to live with and serve.

It is true, of course, that evangelical Christians will use their religious faith to determine where they stand on a number of political issues, but we have no desire to implement the Bible as a book of laws and to force everyone to live according to that code. Forcing people under threat of law to behave in certain ways will not make them Christians anyway, and will not gain them access to heaven. Christians want the government to protect people from one another, especially protecting minorities and those without political and economic power from evil people and those with concentrated power (thus, our noted struggles against things such as slavery and abortion).

God did set up a religious government for the Hebrews when they came out of Egypt to form their own nation (starting in the book of Exodus in the Old Testament). God's plan at that point in history was for His chosen people to have a set of religious laws enforced. Their religious leaders and political leaders were essentially the same people. But this is not what the New Testament calls for now, and this *is not* what those holding a biblical worldview want today in America. Any time church leaders in other countries have officially gathered political power to themselves, it has ended badly for that church. In fact, this is the case with all people who are exposed to political power. That is the reason that we believe in setting term limits on elected officials, and why the answer to question #1 at the beginning of this chapter is "c." If one person, political party, or any other organization (a religious faction, the military, etc.) maintains political power for too long, it always ends badly.

A biblical worldview warns us not to be a one-party people. We desire to have our voices heard by both parties and do not wish for our support (or lack of support) to be taken for granted by either party. We truly believe things will work out best for the country if we sprinkle candidates from both parties at the local, state, and national levels. Political scientists and historians have noted that two of the best episodes in the last one hundred years were when the Republican Ronald Reagan was president and the Speaker of the House of Representatives, Tip O'Neill, was a Democrat, and when the Democrat Bill Clinton was president and Newt Gingrich, a Republican, was speaker of the House.

It may be time for a warning to be sent out to my bible-believing brothers and sisters. Over the past few decades many with a biblical worldview have voted almost exclusively Republican. The main issue driving this is abortion. Something similar happened in American history before. Throughout the early portion of the 1800s, Democrats made slavery a more and more prominent component of their platform. Those with a biblical worldview knew that slavery was flat-out wrong (more on why we believe this later in the chapter). Then the Republican Party was founded to stop the spread of slavery (and soon enough changed its mandate to eliminating slavery all together) and the Bible-thumpers just felt as though they had to align themselves almost exclusively with this new party. Over time, though, Republican politicians such as Herbert Hoover, Reed Smoot, Strom Thurmond, Richard Nixon, and Arlen Specter were not at all the type of politicians that Christians desired to support.

Today a similar shift has happened. Again for biblical reasons, we believe that abortion is flat-out wrong. As some in the Democrat Party have made abortion increasingly central to their platform (especially partial-birth abortion, where the legs and torso of the fetus is delivered outside the mother before its skull is punctured with a medical instrument such as scissors, and the child killed, after which the head is also removed from the mother and the child's lifeless body discarded), many Christians have been driven to abandon the party's mainline candidates. But this division also creates an uneasy feeling that the Republican Party is being given too much support.

As an example of how loyalty to one party can end up causing more harm than good, we need look no further than the fate of private labor unions in America. While many question the value (or even legality) of public labor unions for government workers, almost all can agree that labor unions for workers at private companies have served an important role in America's economic history. Government figures show that after World War II, private labor union participation included one out of every three workers employed in the country. But in 2013 those same government statistics reported less than one in fifteen workers were members of a labor union. Over that same period of time, private labor unions have come to almost exclusively endorse the Democratic Party.

Over the last few decades, as labor unions have supported candidates such as Barack Obama with millions and millions of campaign dollars, their roll sheets have been shrinking. The more membership falls, the more they throw support toward a single party. I believe this has been a huge mistake. Democratic opposition to initiatives such as the Keystone pipeline (with all the direct energy-related jobs and associated indirect manufacturing jobs) has kept private unions from being able to halt their decline.

And so it could be with evangelical Christians. If we decide that we will only engage Republicans (because they are currently saying more of

what we like to hear) and will be intentionally spiteful regarding Democrats (because they are now part of the "other team"), we will hamstring
ourselves and limit our long-term political influence. Instead, I suggest
those with a biblical worldview engage Democrats as well as Republicans at the local, state, and national levels. We are for God and His
work. We are not here to be for or against any one political party.

Political Leaders

There is a verse in the Old Testament wisdom-book of Proverbs which
is important to those with a biblical worldview relative to the traits we
desire in our political leaders: "Where there is no prophetic vision the
people cast off restraint" (Prov. 29:18). Interestingly, this verse seems
to be teaching that it is important for leaders to have strategic vision
regarding the entities they lead, being able to relay that vision to those
under them. But it is actually making a statement much stronger than
that. Verse 18 comes right in the middle of verses about child discipline
and dealing with unproductive workers. What the writer is saying is
that not giving structure to your child, or not holding your workers
accountable, is as ridiculous as a leader not having a strategic vision
he or she can impart to their people. The Bible takes it as a fact of life,
which needs no explanation or defense, that leaders must be strategic
visionaries and not simply those who react as events occur around them.

Any organization of people—a sports team, business, local community, state, or entire country—needs direction from the top. If each
player on a soccer, football, or basketball team runs whatever scheme
or play they desire, the team will fail miserably. Not only does a coach
need to call the schemes and plays so that all the players are working
together (common or traditional leadership), but the coach needs to
have prepared their team to execute the types of schemes and plays that
were most likely to be needed given the opponent they are playing that
week (strategic leadership).

A government leading its citizens is no different. Leaders who can
confidently lead in times of crisis are good (traditional leaders). Leaders
who can foresee crises and limit their negative impact, before leading

confidently through whatever effects remained, are great (strategic leaders). I have heard Christians speaking about this concept use simple descriptions such as "We want our elected leaders to understand the indirect benefits of their direct policies," "We want our elected officials to be able to consider and explain the trade-offs between passing and not passing the legislation," or "We need our leaders to be able to see the trouble brewing on the horizon that the average citizen is going to miss."

A well-known example of good strategic political vision is Winston Churchill's outspoken concern about the growing military threat from Nazi Germany. Even the leaders of his own party in Great Britain could not see what a menace Hitler's Germany was becoming, or how quickly and intentionally it was becoming that menace. Churchill proved to be exactly right with his intuitive concern about the Nazis, but he was not in a political position of power and able to act until it was too late. In a case of poor visionary leadership, the US seemed to have been completely caught off guard when Pearl Harbor was attacked on December 7, 1941. Given Japan's other aggressive military moves up to that point, and the fact that our relations with Japan were in shambles by then (over arguments about their occupation of China, etc.), even the teacher of a high-school civics class should not have been caught flat-footed by the turn of events. It was the difference in their leadership quality of strategic insight that allowed Churchill to see something long before others did, and that caused Roosevelt to miss seeing something that everyone else was becoming weary about.

A slightly more modern example of good strategic intuition was President Reagan's lead on the collapse of the Soviet Union. When he took office in the early 1980s, no human being in the world seemed to think that the Soviets could be bullied, much less bullied into submission, other than Ronald Reagan. As a college student I remember reading article after article that the US was going to provoke Russia and that it would be all Reagan's fault. Our actions were going to force them to respond in unpleasant but unnecessary ways. As it turned out, of course, Reagan had a deep insight into the economic and military susceptibility of the Soviet Socialist Republic. He saw their weakness when few others did, and acted to take advantage of it for the benefit of America and the rest of the world.

A more modern case of poor visionary leadership in the US was when Bill Clinton allowed Osama bin Laden to be released from Sudan to Afghanistan. The Sudanese government had physical control of bin Laden but they were kicking him out of their country in 1996. They said they would turn him over to America but that if we did not want him, they had secured a place to send him in Afghanistan. Of course, the story ends badly. Clinton did not have the strategic foresight of Churchill or Reagan, and declined to take him into custody. The Sudanese did in fact pack him up and ship him to Afghanistan—and the rest, as they say, is history. There is simply no reason, given his record of activities and his endless threats against the West, that we should not have taken him into custody. Poor strategic leadership can literally be deadly. For more detail on this episode from Clinton's presidency, read *The Looming Tower* by Lawrence Wright and *Losing bin Laden* by Richard Miniter.

Perhaps the worse modern case of all was that after what the US and the world went through with bin Laden, American leadership stood by and let it happen again in Syria and Iraq. Our president called this new terrorist organization, ISIS, a JV team and failed to take the small proactive steps that would have been necessary to throttle them. That is simply unacceptable for America's elected leaders.

Though those with a biblical worldview look for evidence of strategic or visionary leadership in our elected officials, we do not think that we are electing perfect men and women, and we do not have the expectation that they will be able to fix every problem which arises. We understand the limitations of humans and see even the president of the United States as just another person, limited by all that makes us human. Evangelicals want to see leaders with insight—and we want the press and the American people to hold those leaders accountable for the things they promise to us, and for the preventable things which transpire that they did not attempt to mitigate—but we do not think that elected officials are there to "save" us, and we do not think they can fix everything.

We not only seek to vote for politicians who have strategic insight but who also have the courage to address the issues. The growing problems of the national debt and the future commitments implied in Social Security and Medicare are not understood by all, and almost no politicians have the courage to be direct with the American people about them. While it can be beneficial for a federal government to have some outstanding debt, America is quickly passing the point of no return. Federal politicians often use deficits in government spending as a campaign issue against one another, but America is at the point where our outstanding debt and the unfunded promises we have made to our senior citizens are no longer minor issues to be pulled out of the bag during election season and then ignored thereafter. They have slowly become the most important issues on the slate. The problem is simple arithmetic; every elected official should understand it. The issue is that there are no easy solutions, so it has become customary in the nation's capital to just look the other way and hope the problem goes away, or to wait for a magic solution to appear over the horizon.

Political Areas Lacking Consensus Agreement

There are two areas where Christians do not always agree. As mentioned earlier in the book, it is the weight given to the Bible and its directives that give us such common understanding and such similar viewpoints. Where the Bible is silent, however, those with a biblical worldview are all over the board.

There is always a debate within the Christian community concerning the weight we should assign to the personal or moral character of our elected leaders. As with most Americans, we would love for the brightest people with the best ideas and most dynamic leadership qualities to also be sin-free choir boys. The hard reality, though, is that history shows some of our best leaders (not just in politics but in business, the military, etc.) do not always have the cleanest records. When leaders are being chosen in a church (elders and deacons, for example), the only two things that matter are their knowledge of the Scriptures and their personal virtues. And that is the way it should be. In fact, in most evangelical churches, when elders or deacons are ordained, they agree that if there is some violation of the Bible's moral code on their part, they will voluntarily step down from the position. Within the church, it is a very black-and-white issue. All people are welcome into the church (murderers, thieves, whoever), but only those who agree that their greatest desire is to live a Christ-like life going forward (the past doesn't matter) will be considered for leadership positions. The New Testament books of 1 Timothy and Titus help us with our understanding of church-leadership requirements.

The contentious issue is to what degree evangelicals should hold politicians to the same standards. Some Christians are convinced that we should only vote for those with similar beliefs (no Mormons, Jews, or maybe even Catholics) and should consider the person's moral fiber more important than their ability to lead in times of crisis or to facilitate economic growth and poverty reductions. While I am very leery of politicians who use heavy-handed tactics against their political enemies (such as the FBI files found in the Nixon White House or the IRS scandal under the Obama administration), I do not think it necessary for every politician for whom I vote to have graduated from a theological seminary and have a spot-proof record. Jimmy Carter is a believing, practicing Christian—and he was also one of our worst presidents. People suffered under his leadership and I simply would not want him or anyone like him to be elected to office ever again. Conversely, and though he stumbled early in his presidency, the Catholic womanizer John F. Kennedy had very promising economic and foreign policy platforms underway by the time he was assassinated. Reagan had been divorced and Carter had not when they ran against each other in 1980, but to me the difference in their leadership abilities far outweighed (in Reagan's favor) the difference in their personal lifestyles.

I personally feel as though I need to weigh leadership qualities very highly relative to a candidate's personal beliefs and indiscretions. Economic crises and wars have caused such hardship throughout history that a political leader with the qualities to navigate those environments is very important to me. Of course, all other things being equal, I would choose the most upstanding individual because character is still important. And my conscience (even if not the Bible) would not allow me to choose even the most brilliant and gifted leader if they were overtly racist, sexist, or involved in some activity that was obviously harmful to society such as child abuse or routinely assaulting others when they got angry.

These decisions are very personal. We have limited direction from the Bible, and therefore you will see us all over the map on our requirements for a political candidate's personal background. This split was vivid and quite public during the 2016 presidential primaries and general election. Russell Moore, the head of the Southern Baptist Convention's Ethics & Religious Liberty Convention, spoke and wrote openly in challenging evangelicals who he thought were too quick to throw support to Donald Trump despite what he saw as Mr. Trump's moral failings.

Our opinions also vary on the degree to which we should be actively lobbying for "moral" causes in the political arena and how we should lobby for those causes. Some moral causes are biblically open-and-shut (such as slavery and abortion) because one group of people is, through force, harming another group which has no way outside of government interference to protect and defend themselves. Given this, we encouraged the government to step in and stop slavery, just as we now encourage the government to step in on abortion.

But outside of those black-and-white issues, some Christians believe that our time and resources are better spent spreading the good news of Jesus Christ and directly helping those who have the greatest needs through religious charities. They believe that the time and money spent on trying to influence the culture around us (especially through political action) could be more wisely invested in the church and those the church is directed to help. A growing number in the evangelical community have called for a halt to our participation in the so-called culture wars, because they believe our efforts have been less than stellar and that we run the risk of not only losing focus but also giving ourselves a questionable name in the community. If we are not looked upon as people who care deeply about those outside the church, our effectiveness at doing what Christ has directed us to do is directly diminished. Their concern is that the more we are seen as driven by politics and what could be mistaken as a self-righteous stand on the public culture, the less opportunity we will have to gain a private audience with those outside the faith. Many other Christians with a biblical worldview, however, quote the fact that Jesus told His followers that they will be the salt and light in the world. Some understand this to mean that we are to expose things which are harmful in the culture (light) and preserve things which are morally valuable in our culture (salt). In order to do this, they argue we must be active in the culture wars, using public forums and political leverage as other organizations do.

Because Christians have a good track record of positively impacting the plight of humans who seem to have little hope of bettering their own situations (orphans, prisoners, slaves, etc.), many evangelicals today say we should still be active in trying to influence the moral sensitivities of the culture around us and, at a minimum, affecting the implementation of laws protecting one subpopulation of citizens from the harm of another. Christians who argue for an ongoing involvement in trying to influence moral issues through political and cultural leverage cite not only the tremendous benefit that has been brought to society by those Christians who have labored recently and in times past. Many times the general population, though critical at first of many of the issues Christians were championing, ultimately came to agree about the immoral nature of many of the elements of society we have worked to change. For example, consider John Howard and his efforts at prison reform in Europe in the 1700s. Today we would be appalled if prisons were run the way they were 250 years ago, and all citizens would demand change. When Howard began his pleas for transformation, however, ordinary citizens did not see the brutal treatment of prisoners as a moral outrage. Many know the story of John Newton who, after a mischievous and delinquent childhood and time spent as the captain of a slave ship, became a Christian and worked for the end of the Atlantic slave trade in Europe. Of course, another famous Christian, William Wilberforce, worked as an elected politician in Great Britain to change the laws of the slave trade, as the likes of Newton and other private Christian citizens created the moral outrage over the issue. In more recent times, we saw elected officials in America, starting with presidents Harry Truman and John F. Kennedy, work the political process from the inside to change the country's laws on race and equal rights, as private Christian citizens, such as the Reverend Martin Luther King, Jr. and the Reverend Ralph David Abernathy Sr., worked to create moral sensitivity to the issue from outside the official political bodies.

Of course, before there were civil-rights issues to be highlighted by Christians and legislated by politicians, there was the issue of slavery in America. The same process happened here as in the cases mentioned above. Conservative Christians became morally outraged at the issue of slavery (based on biblical teachings highlighted later in this chapter). As they first began to agitate the public about the issue, the watchdogs of the cultural standards in those days (journalists, writers, politicians, and judges) were highly critical that the Jesus freaks were sticking their noses where they did not belong, being unnecessarily judgmental of the mainstream culture and trying to have their own morality coded into law. Because these Christians did not see the issue of slavery as an opinion but one of absolute moral wrong based on one human violating the God-given rights of another human, they pressed on through the criticism and threats, trying to build a public groundswell to encourage or force the government to do its job (of protecting people's rights from being violated by other people).

Some of the names of believers who were involved in trying to stop the Atlantic slave trade, promoting the Underground Railroad, or trying to eliminate slavery altogether—such as Harriet Tubman, Frederick Douglass and William Lloyd Garrison—are very well known even by those with little interest in history. But the movements in America to provide passage and safety to runaway slaves and to end the institution itself were founded and funded and energized by Christians with a biblical worldview from the very beginning. We saw blacks as the instrumental figures in the civil rights movement of the 1950s and 1960s. But in the 1850s and 1860s there were not enough free, educated blacks to make a difference. Of course, politicians did not care, because blacks did not vote. And so, thankfully, those with a biblical worldview decided they would have to influence the culture around them in a positive way. At a later point, elected politicians such as Abraham Lincoln and Thaddeus Stevens began to work from inside political bodies to try and change the laws reflecting their constituents' new moral sensitivities.

It should be noted that the more "liberal" denominations and congregations (those which relied less on the Bible and more on traditions and human understanding) were not uniformly antislavery, and in some cases intentionally misused the Bible to try and justify slavery. They were influenced by their own opinions, economic concerns, social biases, personal prejudices, and the pressure of the culture around them. In hindsight, most of those denominations have admitted they should have done more to confront the issue of slavery and regret the fact that they let the cultural and social biases of the times influence them. Having stuck to their biblical beliefs in spite of being harassed by politicians, judges, journalists, and businessmen—and seeing the bulk of the country later come to realize that slavery was a moral evil, just as they had said all along—those with a biblical worldview are as determined as ever to not let ever-changing cultural and social moods influence their efforts to enact what the Bible dictates. We are as determined as ever to earnestly seek in the pages of the Bible what instructions God provides for us on such issues.

As stated, although those with our worldview agree that we want the Bible to be the basis of our moral foundation (and not the whims of the prevailing attitudes of those around us), there will always be a division of opinion between those who believe we should actively try and influence—through both social agitation and political legislation—the prevailing culture around us, and those who believe that is not our role in society, except on major issues of majorities discriminating against minorities. As is also the case now, not all those in the past with a biblical worldview believed in being politically active in the moral and cultural issues of the day. Even some of the black-and-white issues they wanted left to the politicians. For example, a famous preacher, Alexander Campbell, who worked during the era leading up to and including the Civil War, said "I have always been anti-slavery but never an abolitionist." He believed that slavery was a moral and social evil, but he thought the energies of Christians were better spent on trying to re-center the Bible as the foundation of the church and working on unifying all the various denominations of New Testament churches. For Campbell, Christians should have voted for Lincoln and then let him, as a politician, deal with the political issue of slavery.

Making Laws: The Spectrum of Choice and Balancing the Scale

If a vote was put before the citizens of a state on how old someone had to be to get a driver's license, or how fast cars should be allowed to legally drive on the highway, a biblical worldview would not play a role in determining how one would vote. These are still moral decisions, of course—all laws are legislated morality—they are just not moral decisions based directly on the Bible. But Christians still have a view as to how making these choices should be framed. In these cases, it is helpful, rather than trying to debate issues on a black-and-white basis (as human nature drives us to do), to consider and debate them along the spectrum of possibilities. For example, the age for obtaining a driver's license could be debated (by citizens or politicians running for office) based on the following spectrum:

Minimum Legal Age to Obtain a Driver's License

Age 14	Age 15	Age 16	Age 17	Age 18

A more controversial moral decision involves what types of weapons individuals should be able to legally own. The debate is not framed by a simple yes or no concerning whether citizens should be allowed to own guns. Honest citizens and politicians have to discuss the (morality of the) issue along a wide spectrum of possibilities. Again, though, one's belief in the Bible has no direct bearing on which option would be chosen.

Type of Weapon Which Can Be Legally Owned

No Weapons Air Rifles Shotguns Rifles Pistols Automatic Weapons

There have also been recent debates about which types of relationships should be granted the benefits of a legally recognized marriage. I have heard no politician suggest that people of the same gender cannot have relationships with each other and/or live together. But a marriage is first and foremost a religious institution, and this must be given weight in the discussions. Given this, Christians mostly want to maintain the biblical definition of marriage in the political arena. The legal aspect of marriage conveys certain rights and tax benefits initially designed to promote families, primarily assisting them in child-rearing. Most libertarians say that no one should be allowed any legal or tax benefits for marriage. They believe that marriage is a religious institution only, and that the state should not officially recognize any marriage or marriage-type relationship for any reason. Libertarians agree that people should be able to form whatever personal or romantic relationships they desire, of course. In their insightful book *Nudge*, Richard H. Thaler and Cass R. Sunstein propose a compromise which should be appealing to all. In their chapter called "Privatizing Marriage," they propose that marriage become (again) a strictly religious institution, administered only by religious organizations. The government would provide legal recognition of, and certain rights to, what they call civil unions. Would you agree with Thaler and Sunstein (as I do) that this proposal—because it preserves the religious aspect of marriage while allowing a separate legal recognition to all—deserves greater discussion? If not, and you would keep the two combined as they are now, where would you draw the line on the spectrum below and why?

Relationships Granted Legal Status of Marriage

No Type of Relationship	One Man One Woman	One Person of One Gender & Multiple People of Opposite Gender	Two People of the Same Gender	Multiple People of Mixed Genders

Another tricky issue which should be framed and debated along a spectrum involves the right of free speech. Again, the Constitution protects our right to criticize and question the government, as individuals or organizations. But the issue is not black-and-white. The voters in a democracy will also have the right to put parameters on how that free speech is utilized. The spectrum for such a discussion might include, on one end, any type of speech or protest desired (including shouting from loud speakers at three in the morning while driving through your neighborhood), to the other end where only written protests are allowed to be published and no group gatherings or spoken protests are allowed. Those on the one end of the spectrum might argue that free speech is too important to infringe upon in any way, and that if your neighbors decide to blast out criticisms of the government while you are sleeping you will just have to adjust. Those on the other end of the spectrum might argue that people can express their opinions without infringing so much on others, and that allowing groups of people to congregate and protest would be too likely to lead to a riot and injuries to people and property. There is no right or wrong in this case. Citizens have to be allowed some free and effective way to voice their opinions (and especially disagreements) about political and legal matters but every option, whether burning flags or burning crosses, does not have to remain open. The options along the spectrum should be established and discussed, and then whatever the majority votes for wins.

When discussing political matters that we cannot all agree on based on biblical mandates, another common-sense framework those with a biblical worldview like to use is balancing the likely benefits and costs of a particular type of action. Too many politicians, and almost all those in the press, frame and discuss issues as if their opinions have no costs and that differing opinions have no possible benefits. The Bible teaches us that in this imperfect world there will always be direct and indirect benefits, and costs and drawbacks, which need to be plainly stated and weighed out when making political decisions. America is not doing this well in our political discourse today. Neither the politicians running for office nor the press corps covering them are facilitating discussions around the real tradeoffs of our toughest political choices.

An illustration from the past would be when the production and consumption of alcohol was outlawed in the United States. Because it is an addictive substance which has destroyed many lives, it is no great surprise that outlawing it was considered. However, when making any political decision, we have to think about unintended consequences and any drawbacks associated with each choice. As an oversimplified example, the balance between the costs and benefits of outlawing alcohol is demonstrated in the graph below.

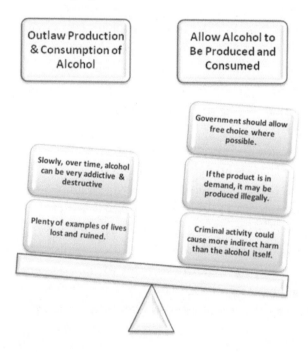

The debate over illegal drugs should be framed in the same manner. Though it can certainly make one feel righteous to oppose the legalization of any drugs, all the direct and indirect costs and benefits should be weighed before continuing with or changing current policy. I believe the balance of the scale could tip either way on this one, and that a new, honest debate about our drug laws and policies should be opened in America today. I have seen firsthand the destruction that drugs cause in our society. The negative impacts on drug users and their families are usually much quicker and more pronounced than those same effects on the users of alcohol. However, we are spending billions of dollars on eradicating the drug trade, with little to show for the effort. There is a huge toll taken on law enforcement in terms of time and money spent, prisons are overflowing with those convicted of (minor) drug offenses, and drug cartels in foreign countries wreak havoc on millions of lives in their efforts to serve America's drug appetite. What should be the considerations stacked on either side of the balance in reconsidering America's drug policy? In which direction do the scales tip in your opinion, and why?

Another example of how those with a biblical worldview would frame a contentious modern political debate involves the treatment of illegal immigrants in America today. Specifically, let's discuss whether children brought to the US illegally by someone else (the so-called Dreamers) should be allowed the same educational opportunities as those of citizens, especially admission to public state colleges at the discounted rate available to in-state, legal residents' children. This is a heated topic of discussion at the local, state, and federal level every time an election cycle rolls around, and especially in the 2016 presidential election. As with so many other topics, those who fall on either side of the debate tend to paint their position on the matter as obviously right and those who disagree with them as obviously wrong.

You may place different considerations on the scale, but all should agree that this is not a black-and-white issue with a single, morally correct solution. There are pluses and minuses to be weighed. Personally, I believe children who were brought into the country illegally by their parents should have an equal opportunity to a college education,

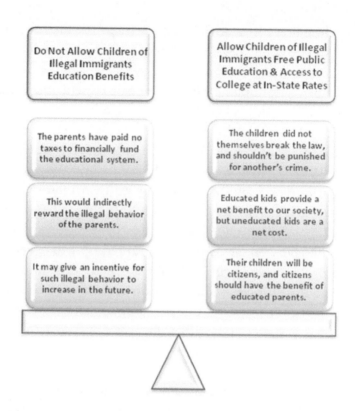

including all the financial benefits available to citizens and legal residents. Part of the reason I feel this way is that in the not-too-distant future, America will lack for young workers to drive our economy and provide the tax revenues to support our Social Security and Medicare benefits. Labor-force participation has been trending down in the US. And as we can see from other developed countries such as France and Japan, a lack of young, educated workers coming into the workforce is a nearly insurmountable economic problem. It is a total waste of a young person's life to not allow them every opportunity to achieve their highest possible level of education and productiveness in the workforce, and it is a huge lost opportunity for America to not leverage all of the smart young people (peacefully) residing within our borders, educating them and benefiting from their inventiveness, productivity, and tax revenue.

In weighing out the options, I tip the scale in favor of providing educational benefits (including college and professional schools) to the children of illegal immigrants. But this stance is not based directly on the teachings of the Bible, and if you have honestly weighed the relevant options and drawn a different conclusion, we should be able to respectfully disagree without calling each other monsters.

Decisions Guided by Our Faith

The moral principles in the Bible do not determine how I vote on every issue. Again, as examples, the legal age at which someone should be allowed to drive and the types of guns which can be privately owned are based more on the constitution and personal experience than anything else. For those with a biblical worldview, however, the Bible does singularly determine where we stand and therefore how we vote on certain issues. Not every position has an obvious right and an obvious wrong, but the Bible clearly says that some things *are* right and some things wrong in how humans deal with each other. We see the purpose of the law as being to protect individuals from an overreaching government and from being harmed by their neighbors. The Bible says that it is a sin for me to cuss while I am alone in my room, but this would not harm my neighbor so we do not believe it is under the jurisdiction of what the government should legislate. The Bible says that if I give money to Jane only so Jim will think that I am a better person than John, then that is a sin. These types of inner thought and motive issues define the majority of what is prescribed by Jesus and His apostles to govern our behavior as Christians. I cannot overstress enough, though, that evangelical Christians do not want to code all of these sinful thoughts and actions as being against the law.

For example, the Bible does not say that it is a sin (for someone of legal age) to drink alcohol. In fact, God established festivals in the Old Testament which included drinking alcohol; Jesus drank wine; and the apostle Paul wrote to one of his appointed church leaders, Timothy, that he should drink a little wine occasionally because of an anxious stomach and frequent ailments (1 Tim. 5:23). But there are two classes of folks who would prefer to have alcohol and its consumption outlawed. The first group consists of those individuals who say that drinking is wrong and should be condemned by the government. Disrespecting your mom is also wrong but I am not sure I want the government trying to impose criminal penalties for every smart-mouthed teenager who disrespects his or her parents. The second group would be those who say that drinking can too easily become a problem for the drinker. There are millions of people today, and millions more throughout history, who have ruined their lives with alcohol. They say it is a strong, addictive substance and that the government should outlaw drinking in order to save people from themselves. But we simply do not see that as the government's role. Many more people have ruined their lives through anger and bitterness, but I don't see how we can outlaw that. There are many people who eat the wrong types of food (too much sugar or fat), or fail to get any exercise, and those decisions have large, cumulative, negative effects on their health as well, but I don't want to pay for an ice-cream sheriff to patrol my neighborhood.

Continuing with our example of drinking, let's expand a bit on how a biblical worldview impacts the role we see for the government. Without question, we would want everyone who committed an act of violence or theft against another person when they were drunk to be held criminally (and civilly) liable for his or her actions. It is fine if the legal penalties for things such as theft and assault are greater if the perpetrator is intoxicated than if they are not (in much the same way that some localities enforce greater penalties for armed robberies if the gun is actually loaded). Governments must punish people who harm one another, especially physically through force or financially through deception. Almost everyone, Christians and non-Christians alike, believes that governments should proactively restrain people from harming one another. The tricky part becomes: When is someone so likely to harm another that we can impose legal force to stop it, although the harm has not yet occurred (and might possibly never occur)? The overwhelming majority of Christians agree that drunk driving should be illegal and enforced with stiff penalties. Of course, many people drive drunk and never harm anyone. But we simply believe that the risk that they will ultimately harm someone else is just too great. In other words, getting drunk is a sin, and harming someone while drunk is a sin. But because being drunk should not be illegal (see balance graph above), and harming someone while drunk should be illegal (because that is an absolute wrong), the question of whether driving drunk should be illegal is a balance question. Again, not everyone who drives intoxicated will ultimately harm someone else, but I would shift the balance to making it illegal after I consider all the positive and negative factors. As a Christian, I understand that you may—considering the positive and negative factors, as well as direct and unintended consequences which you think are most relevant—develop opinions which are the opposite of mine (i.e., that drinking should be illegal, or that driving drunk should be legal). But our Bible-driven morality tells us that we cannot budge on the fact that a drunk person harming another person should be illegal.

Where one human will or very likely could physically or financially harm another human, we believe laws should be put into place and enforced. Murder, rape, robbery, assault, fraud, driving drunk, and similar activities should be against the law. The apostle Paul tells us that God has ordained the function of a government to be enforcing exactly those types of laws (Rom. 13:1–7).

Let me give an example of why using the Bible as our foundation is so important to us. Historically, when humans rely on measures other than a constant set of beliefs, they are tempted to change their political decisions based on personal motives of greed, popularity, etc. Again, the two most controversial cases to be put forth as examples in this realm are slavery and abortion. I say controversial because opposition to abortion and slavery have not always been the majority opinion, and Christians have been ruthlessly ridiculed by atheists, politicians, and those in the press who disagree with us. But based on a biblical worldview, one must be and must have always been opposed to both. Slavery and abortion are not issues to be weighed in the balance with competing factors, causing different individuals to reach different conclusions. These issues involve one set of humans completely determining the fate of another set of humans, through no fault of their own and without their consent. The Bible teaches us that we are supposed to implement government in such a way as to prevent exactly that from happening. In contrast to this, the original political activists who we would call liberals today (including Thomas Jefferson, who has been called the father of the modern-day Democrat Party) were all opposed to abortion, yet in favor of slavery. Today, because the political pressure on the two issues has flipped, liberals are opposed to slavery and mostly in favor of abortion. We believe that it is very dangerous for people with the same political philosophy to have such radically different views on such critically important life-and-death topics based on anything other than an absolute standard. We cannot allow things as drastic as slavery to be determined by popular opinion, or by whether I see any personal benefit for it.

Our biblical worldview determines the stand we take on these types of issues, and we do not deny that our point of view is derived from our understanding of God's word revealed in the Bible. Students of history know that it was Christians in Great Britain and America who led the charge for the end of slavery. There are a few main verses in the Bible which led them to take this moral stand. I should note that the verses in the Bible about slavery have probably been more intentionally abused than those on any other topic, by both sides of the fight. Centuries ago slave owners, "Southern Democrats," and most newspaper editors relied on the fact that some forms of slavery existed in the Bible to (incorrectly) justify the type of slavery which then existed in America. Today, many who are opposed to the very concept of God or Christianity, in trying to show that the Jews and their God are bad, cite the fact that the Old Testament actually had laws regulating slavery. There absolutely were various forms of slavery in the Bible, just as there are various forms today. Some of the terms are different and some of the applications have been modified, but forms of involuntary servitude existed then and now. Prisoners of war were held as "slaves" in the Old Testament, meaning that they were taken captive and were no longer allowed the freedom to choose where to go or what to do. Today we take prisoners of war captive, and do not allow them to go where they want or do what they want either. Prisoners of war are held captive against their will, and every aspect of their lives are regulated and controlled by someone else.

Some "slaves" in the Bible were under a term of servitude to their master because they owed an amount of money which they could not pay back according to the original terms. In working for the master, they were "forced" to have the fruits of their labor go to repay what they owed. The history books tell us that as a boy Abraham Lincoln served as such a temporary slave worker to an individual, to whom his father owed money which he was unable to repay. The system has changed but we still have the concept. Today, there are millions of people whose wages are garnished for payment to someone whom they owe but could not or would not pay under the terms of the original agreement or court order. These individuals in America are involuntarily having the fruit of their labor (or at least a portion of it) taken away and given to someone else. By one of the Old Testament definitions, they are slaves. Other examples of slavery in the Old Testament involve people willingly selling themselves into servitude (and then deciding later on if they wanted to stay under the employment of their boss). Is that not similar to an athlete signing on with a sports team and being contractually obligated to play for just them, or to an entertainer signing a contract committing themselves to only recording songs for a certain label?

If so many forms of involuntary servitude were witnessed in the Bible and so many similar forms still exist today, why have those with a biblical worldview been saying for the last four hundred years that the type of slavery practiced in America was wrong? We opposed it then and now very simply because the Bible expressly forbids the idea of kidnapping and forcing an innocent person into slavery, and that is the system that America copied from the Arab and European nations hundreds of years ago. The thirteenth amendment to the Constitution, which explicitly outlawed that type of slavery in the US, made sure to clarify exactly the type of involuntary servitude (or slavery) it was prohibiting:

Neither slavery nor involuntary servitude, except as a punishment for crime whereof the party shall have been duly convicted, shall exist within the United States, or any place subject to their jurisdiction.

The verses which cause those with a biblical worldview to believe that the form of slavery which existed in America should be illegal are:

- Exodus 21:16
- Deuteronomy 15:12–18
- Deuteronomy 24:7
- 1 Timothy 1:10

In 1 Timothy, Paul condemns (among other things) an act or profession that would be translated into English as "an enslaver, a kidnapper or man stealer, a slave trader." No one with a biblical worldview could have supported slavery for a moment. But in the newspapers of the day, the reporters and editors told the Bible-thumpers that they should shut up and stop trying to enforce their beliefs on others. I do not want to enforce all my moral opinions on others but I absolutely believe that I should stand up for people who have no ability to stand up for themselves, when what is being perpetrated against them is an absolute moral wrong and not just an opinion of mine. There is no moral spectrum and no balancing of issues with the type of slavery which existed in the United States. It was and is an absolute wrong, because the Bible says so!

In today's world, of course, the hot-button issue is abortion. I understand that all Americans want control over their own bodies, and we all believe we have a right to make personal decisions without the interference of the government. Our rights stop, though, where the rights of another individual begin. Sometimes this is very loosely defined, such as when young men are drafted into the Armed Forces to serve and protect the country in a time of war. The government's moral argument here is essentially that you have privileges as a citizen, and that those privileges are being threatened by a foreign armed force; therefore, the young men most capable of fighting should be required by the government to risk their bodies and their lives in defending the rights of fellow citizens. My rights (to avoid fighting in wars that I did not start) get infringed upon by my own government, so that the rights of others do not get infringed upon by foreign governments. The logic that my rights end where another person's rights begin gets pretty stretched here, quite frankly. Nevertheless, when I was eighteen years old, I went down and signed up with the Selective Service. It was the legal thing to do, and I believe it was also biblically the right thing to do.

The moral argument against slavery and abortion is much more straightforward: The life of another human being is involved, and your rights stop where theirs begins. If you are a slave owner, you must set the slave free. If you are pregnant with a child, you must carry it to term and give birth. I understand that many slaveholders had spent all their money buying up other people and were financially ruined when they were forced to set their slaves free. But I just cannot get past the point that the slave was another human being—equal in God's eyes to the owner and therefore equally deserving of freedom. Likewise, I understand that some pregnant women do not desire to be pregnant but I cannot get past the fact that the embryo is a child—equal in God's eyes to the mother and therefore equally deserving of a chance at life.

Interestingly, probably a near-majority of evangelical Christians with whom I have personally spoken have no problem allowing for the option of abortion where the mother's life is in certain danger from a term pregnancy (their argument being that in that case the baby—through no fault of its own—is threating the life of the mother and, therefore, can have its rights infringed upon), but none of them can cite an example where they have known such a risk to actually be the case.

The entire Bible teaches of the specialness and sanctity of human life. Even a cursory reading would convince one of the immoralities of the act of abortion. A few specific scriptures, though, tell us that the child inside the womb is a living human deserving equal rights to all of us outside the womb:

- Exodus 21:22–23, 25
- Psalm 139:13–14
- Luke 1:41–45

As in the past, politicians, professors, entertainers, newspaper colum-
nists, and TV-show anchors tell those with a biblical worldview to be
quiet and stop trying to force our morals down everyone's throat. They
say this is either because society tells them that this is the more morally
acceptable stand today (just as slavery used to be the morally acceptable
stand for the self-righteous) or because they believe that the sexual revo-
lution (and the nasty outcomes associated with it, such as abortion on
demand and fathers who need not take responsibility for their offspring)
benefits them personally. As we have discussed many times already in
this book, I do not care to make all the things I consider immoral to be
illegal. But when a person or group of people is helpless with no voice for
themselves in the political debate, and has no way to defend themselves
from the harm of others, the Bible teaches I should use the government to
defend them, regardless of the criticism received from the public at large.

Christians believe that some aspects of the law should be influenced
directly by the Bible. Slavery and abortion, for example, involve parties
which are politically connected causing direct harm on unconnected
parties, requiring the government to step into its God-given role of pro-
tector of the weak. We do not believe, however, that everything that is
a sin against God should be regulated or outlawed. We understand that
humans have a natural tendency to make issues too black-and-white,
painting our choice as clearly good and any version of an alternative
choice as clearly bad. Therefore, we encourage political debates to consider the spectrum of choices, and the costs and benefits of each.

Finally, as always, we stand firm that what disproves itself when
tested should be scratched from consideration. The Bible does not
provide detailed answers for every situation, but it does teach us to be
rational in observing and weeding out false prophets in every field and
of every type and description. For example, military dictatorships have
proven to be very unsuccessful forms of government and should not be
considered as a viable option. Political leaders who do not have the strategic insight to accurately discern growing strategic threats have allowed
much harm to be unleashed. Therefore, Christians believe that strategic
insight is a characteristic we should look for in our politicians.

CHAPTER 5

The View of Economics

Would Jesus have been a communist?

    a. Yes

    b. No

The answer is "b," no.

Many people have asked me, "Didn't Jesus tell some rich guy in the Bible that he needed to give all his money to the poor? That sounds like communism to me!" The story they reference is found in Luke 18:18–23, and is not dealing directly with the issue of money. We will return to and explain what Jesus was teaching in those verses shortly. But before we get to that story, let's consider another, less well-known statement Jesus made, which does deal directly with the issue of money and how it is allocated between different people.

> Someone in the crowd said to him, "Teacher, tell my brother to divide the inheritance with me." But he said to him, "Man, who made me a judge or arbitrator over you?" And he said to them, "Take care, and be on your guard against all covetousness, for one's life does not consist in the abundance of his possessions" (Luke 12:13–15).

What? Now we see why Jesus was not universally popular when He was on earth. To tell a rich person that he should not idolize his money or become consumed with greed to make more and more money (which Jesus said to many people on many occasions) will draw a cheer from many in the crowd. But to turn around and tell a person who is not rich that he should not be concerned about equaling out the wealth among people but should be concerned with higher moral matters between man and God would hurt your popularity a bit. And then, to actually tell the non-rich person that his jealousy or envy was as bad as the rich man's greed and idolizing of money would make you downright hated in many places.

The story in Luke 18 that many people misunderstand as Jesus having told someone to be a communist is actually about Jesus instructing someone that they were leaning too much on their wealth to define who they were, and were in essence attempting to buy their righteousness and good standing. This person had his own version of religion, twisted to fit the reality he had made for himself. With his wealth, this young man could make all the guilt and sin offerings at the temple he (thought) he would ever need. Of course, wealth always provides a certain level of social status in any society, and the Jewish society in which this young man was raised seemed to be providing him with a false sense of superior righteousness, to go along with his inflated sense of popularity and worth.

Jesus, however, felt bad for this individual. Though the young man appeared to have it all on the outside, Jesus could clearly tell that there was a struggle raging inside this person. Jesus knew that the start to unraveling the mess of it all was for this person to give up the false crutch that his wealth and recognition gave him superior (moral) status. With that fantasy removed, the young man could then begin to build healthier views of Jesus, religion, and righteousness, and a more appropriate relationship between himself and God. Jesus did not tell every rich person He met to part with their wealth. That was not a standard part of His teaching (though He, and His apostles after Him, did stress to everyone, rich and poor, that money should not be an idol for them). But he had to tell this man to part with his money because it was his crutch; he thought it allowed him righteousness and moral status apart from God.

Jesus told a parable which teaches the same lesson. In Matthew 20:1–16, He tells of workers who were hired first thing in the morning to labor for twelve hours in a vineyard for the owner of an orchard. These workers, knowing they had valuable labor to provide and other options on where to work that day, negotiated a wage rate with the vineyard owner before going to work and earning their pay. As the story goes on, Jesus says that with just one hour to go in the work day, the foreman went back out to hire workers who had been looking for employment all day but had found none. These workers did not negotiate a wage for their labor. They knew that in reality with only one hour left in the work day, they didn't really have much of value to offer and were really relying on the generosity of the vineyard owner to pay them anything at all for their meager labor. Instead, they are paid for the entire day! Jesus closes out that story by saying the first will be last and the last will end up first. By this He simply meant that if we feel our "labor" (what we can do or what we can buy) is worth something before God, we will end up last. But when we realize that what we have to offer in terms of righteousness is too meager to be of any value to God anyway (in a sense, placing ourselves last), then we can begin to see that only through the mercy of Jesus and the cross can we ever obtain a first-place standing.

There are many modern-day examples of the rich young man with whom Jesus had the conversation in Luke 18—those who seek their value as a person, and more importantly gain a sense of goodness or righteousness, from their material possessions. Notoriety and wealth can give us an unhealthy view of our standing in the world. Money and influence can purchase many earthly things. But if we are unwilling to meet the moral identity we need through a relationship with Christ, we may seek to be our own righteousness through the things our money and influence can do. In doing so, however, we have to twist our view of who Jesus is— the rich young man called Jesus good teacher instead of Lord; and a well-known millionaire celebrity once made the statement that Jesus did not come to die on the cross for our sins but only came to give us a different consciousness about how we should live (in other words, He was a good teacher but not their Lord). And this distorts in our minds what our relationship should be with God through Christ. If an individual such as this were to speak to Jesus on the same topic as the young man in the Bible—seeking Jesus' approval for their moral standing based primarily on the good things they had done with their money—he no doubt would respond in much the same way.

So if those with a biblical worldview would not recommend communism as the ideal economic system, what do we support? Capitalism! The reason is very simple. Capitalism has proven historically to be the best system to pull people out of poverty. Remember, Christians are interested in what has been proven true, and what has been shown to actually work, not what makes the best (but often false) promises. Christians do not want people to be poor. We really do not care who is rich, or how rich they get, but it hurts us when people live in poverty. Again, making income and having money is not bad in itself. As with almost anything (alcohol, strong emotions, leisure time), humans can turn something neutral such as how much they earn into a sin (in this case idolatry and greed). But just because something *can* be turned sinful, it does not mean that we should avoid it or have politicians try to legislate around it.

Throughout history, capitalism has shown itself superior when compared to any and every other economic system for pulling people out of poverty, and all the horrible consequences that come with being really poor. A few times in the recent past, history has literally provided us with head-to-head comparisons of capitalism and communism—West vs. East Germany, and South vs. North Korea. Over just a couple of decades, the capitalist country in those cases was so far ahead of the communist country in terms of living standards that the communist countries had to build walls and fences to keep people from escaping to the capitalist country.

Within single countries, we have seen astounding evidence of the power of capitalism in the last few decades. As India and China made aggressive moves toward more capitalist societies, and even though neither is really there yet, literally hundreds of millions of people were given the opportunity to pull themselves out of poverty. More people were taken from the clutches of being painfully poor by the capitalist adjustments made in these two countries than have been pulled out of poverty by all the billions of dollars of foreign aid given to every country over the entire history of the world. Should those of us who have material wealth share with those who do not have as much? Absolutely. But all that giving will never be able to match what a few political and economic changes can make for literally billions of people in the world today. I am not saying that we cannot or should not vote in a democracy to have a social safety net (e.g., unemployment checks for people who lose their jobs suddenly, or financial support to feed young children in poor families) but we should not introduce economic policies in order to give us a clean-feeling conscience if it is going to cause poor people to suffer (more) in the long run.

Without pursuing a degree in economics, it is easy to survey the economic landscape across countries which have varying degrees of capitalist policies in place, and see plenty of evidence that the more capitalist the policies of a country's economic system, the faster poverty is reduced. Have you ever wondered why so many rich Canadians come to the US for advanced medical treatment? Don't they essentially have free medical services available to them in Canada? Yes, but because the government is heavily involved in the Canadian health sector—regulating out many of the capitalistic impulses that would otherwise drive that industry—it fails to serve people as well as the American system does today. (Of course, we do see places where the US government has long been heavily involved in health care, as in the case of veteran care.) For an interesting take on the comparison of health systems, read *Lives at Risk* by John Goodman, Gerald Musgrave, and Devon Herrick.

Of course, many who have followed recent headlines may ask why the US had a much, much worse collapse in her housing market than did Canada. The answer is the reverse of the above. The American government is much more involved in the housing and mortgage markets than the government is in Canada. Between laws designed to force lenders to make certain mortgage loans, and the government-sponsored entities of Freddie Mac and Fannie Mae (which were at the root of the so-called Great Recession America suffered, starting in 2008) to the fact that taxpayers in the US can deduct mortgage interest off their taxes,

America was bound to suffer greater economic losses from our housing market than Canada. Our housing market was less capitalistic, less free of government intrusion and regulation than Canada's. The politicians who implemented all those health-related laws and regulations in Canada, and all the mortgage and housing-related laws and regulations in the US, will of course say that those laws were intended to help. Giving children everything they want may be intended to help children as well but, again, we don't need a degree in child psychology to understand the broad evidence available that giving children everything they want is not a way to make them happy and responsible as they grow.

Without it being anybody's intention, natural experiments have been established over time which clearly demonstrate the superiority of capitalistic policies over those of any other type. Starting with the most extreme cases, after World War II, certain countries were broken into communist and non-communist divisions—for example, East Germany (communist) was divided from West Germany (capitalistic), and North Korea (communist) separated from South Korea (capitalistic). Similar examples would be the differences one sees in comparing mainland China in her purely communist days to Taiwan to Hong Kong. When comparing the economic differences, as well as the rates of poverty and hunger among children, across these countries of identical ethnic and historical makeup, we see the communist countries lose (and lose big) *every single time*. For some reading on this specific subject, I would recommend *Nothing to Envy: Ordinary Lives in North Korea* by Barbara Demick.

Even when we compare countries that are just different in the shade of their capitalistic nature, we get the same results. The more capitalistic the policies of the country, the better off their economic environments. After the collapse of the Soviet Union's empire, countries such as Poland moved more quickly and decisively toward capitalism than did some others such as the Ukraine. These countries were all starting from more or less the same point. Of course, those such as Poland which chose a more capitalistic approach have healthier economies and wealthier citizens than those countries which chose more socialistic methods.

The countries which share the Euro currency went through a severe economic crisis starting in 2008, like much of the rest of the world. Using the premise above that the more a country's economic policies aimed to redistribute wealth or were outright socialistic the worse their economies will do and the poorer their people will be, one would have predicted that Greece would have suffered the most (they have actually elected communists into their Parliament), and that countries such as Italy, Spain, and France would not be far behind. As the drama unfolded (especially in 2011), Eurozone countries began to struggle to pay their debt obligations, and selective government defaults threatened the very existence of the currency union, the countries which fell first and fell hardest were Greece, Italy, and Spain—in that order. The less the governments promoted the tenets of capitalism, the worse their people did.

Before we continue with our discussion of the pros and cons of capitalism, let me define what I mean by the term. Capitalism is simply an economic system which arises when individuals are allowed to pursue their own economic interests in whatever (legal) ways best fit them. Each person or any group of people are allowed to start or close businesses, produce existing or new products, sell to customers within or outside the country, and make as much profit as they (legally) can. The need to feed ourselves and sleep under some form of shelter will cause us to exert working effort and at least gather up useful items that exist in nature. The incentive of making a profit which consistently allows people to provide for themselves beyond just the basic needs of life, improve their standard of living over time, and save up wealth to pass on to their family is what will drive the economy to grow and lift people out of poverty. The Bible speaks of incentives in a number of places. People are not perfect and are not going to act perfectly without some form of incentives (usually both positive and negative). Capitalism leverages natural financial incentives to improve people's lives.

Allow me to use an oversimplified example to make a basic point. If I am hired into a business to produce finished lumber from raw trees, and I am paid the same as every other worker in the plant, I will likely be an average worker like everyone on the job. There is little incentive for me to look at the more experienced workers to see if they have any "tricks of the trade" I could learn and apply, and little incentive to try and come up with my own improvements to how I do my job. If I am going to make $500 a week regardless of what I do, history shows that over the course of my career I will not continue to work harder and smarter for extended periods of time based on just my conscience. It is fine to say that people should work as hard and smart as they can for their employer no matter what (and the Bible does tell Christians to work as though Jesus was our boss on every job), but again past experience tells us that trying to cling to such moral high ground will just cause people to continue living in poverty. In fact, over time in a system with no incentive for improvement, most workers will not only fail to improve the productivity of their labor but will seek to perform at the lowest possible level without being fired.

On the other hand, if I go to work where each worker produces an average of one hundred planks a day and gets paid a dollar per plank, the first thing I will do is try and learn the "tricks of the trade" from the more experienced workers, as well as try and create my own ways of being more productive. I may decide that I want to adopt some children and spend as much time with them as possible, so I work hard and smart for thirty-five or forty hours a week, produce seven hundred planks, and gladly go home with my seven hundred dollars to do the things in life that are more important to me. A coworker, however, may borrow and create every possible ingenious way to produce more and more planks per hour, and then work sixty hours a week. My coworker may make $1,500 a week and would be free in an incentive-based, capitalistic economy to either spend or save their income. My coworker makes more than twice what I make but it is because they work both harder and longer than I do. I decide how to spend my time, and may have decided in my heart that raising adopted children is more important to me than money.

There is another aspect of capitalism that seems obvious to us in America, but is not so matter-of-fact to some others in the world: If my coworker not only has discovered more efficient ways to produce planks from felled trees than all the other employees, but also believes they have seen some ways in which they could run a plank business more efficiently than the current owner, they are free to go start a plank company of their own. If they can in fact produce planks more efficiently than their former employer, they will take their business away by selling the lumber at a cheaper rate. Now the poor farmers in the area can build their barns more cheaply, and keep more of the money; as a result, their farm produces more income or profit. In this example, even though different workers ended up making different amounts of money, the system was fair because each was being paid for what they produced. Instead of everyone sitting around complaining about life and trying to do as little as possible, certain people are trying very hard to be creative and productive, knowing they will get financial rewards if they do.

We are often tempted to speak of the individual who worked those long hours and started a competing business as greedy, or maybe even immoral in some way. But this is not always the case, and society should not label those entrepreneurs in such a way. Suppose that the oldest adopted child is now ready to enter the world on their own and has decided that, based on their skills, desires, and some land they have, they want to be a farmer but could not because the cost of building all the barns and stables and chicken houses would just be too much of a financial load. Enter my old coworker, who allows lumber to be purchased more cheaply, and so the farm becomes economically feasible. Once the farm is producing, they may be able to get food to the local market more cheaply, which would take some pressure off the household budgets of low-income families in the area with multiple children to feed. That example might seem simplistic, but the idea that individual people should have economic freedom to make job and financial decisions based on incentives certainly is not silly. The idea that fairness of opportunity is what matters, not fairness of outcome, is vital to allowing economic growth to pull people out of poverty. And it is biblical.

For as long as there has been capitalism, there has been concern that it produces unequal income among the members of society. There is no doubt that this is true, but in some ways the income inequality is just part of the incentive structure that makes capitalism so successful. As mentioned above, if individuals in society who have gone through some type of advanced education or training do not make more than those with no enhanced skills, people will stop trying to improve themselves and the work they do. That would obviously cause harm to the overall health of the economy and severely limit economic growth. Some people will choose to work as much as possible and to save as much as possible, while others will spend their income as fast as they earn. Of course, those who choose to save will end up over the years with more wealth than the spenders, and all that wealth will earn them extra interest—making their income even higher. But it is not necessarily a bad thing that older workers who have more experience in their jobs, or workers who have completed training, earn more than others. When you think it through, it would seem quite unfair if a twenty-year-old with questionable work habits made as much as a fifty-year-old who has worked hard on their education and has built up a valuable stock of knowledge about the industry they work in and the job which they do. It is helpful if that twenty-year-old can see the monetary value of continuing to train and learn, and to work hard so they can work their way into the financial position of the successful fifty-year-old. As the twenty-year-old decides to become more educated and efficient in their work, all of society will benefit from him or her being a more productive citizen. Before we complain about income inequality, we should remember that older and more skilled workers should make more than younger and less productive workers.

Of course, if some people have higher income and greater wealth than others because they are cheating in some way, Christians would be the first group to throw a flag. The Bible is full of admonitions about unfair business practices. To have the type of dynamic capitalism that lifts people out of poverty a hundred million souls at a time, both the businesses and the government must work in certain ways. It is sad that so many political pundits writing newspaper editorials, or being interviewed on TV, talk about how we must make a choice between greedy pigs running wild over people in an unrestrained capitalistic society with no role for government, or from more of a welfare state where the government keeps one set of people from abusing another and helping to ensure that everything is "fair."

No one who promotes a free capitalist society (whether Christian or atheist) claims that there is no role for the government. Those who are opposed to capitalism, and who claim that those who are in favor of capitalism want no role for government, are simply not telling the truth (and know it). If you think about capitalism as a football game, the government plays the role of the referees. In football, having multiple players for each position on the team helps to ensure that everybody is trying hard to earn playing time on the field. That competition makes the team better, just like workers within a company trying to figure out how to produce more planks than their coworkers makes the overall company better. Of course, as teams play each other, the competition will determine over the course of a season who the best team is in the league, just as competition between businesses will allow their customers to determine which product in the marketplace is better. And just as in football, the competition would be meaningless if there were not rules enforced by the authorities. Each team should be allowed to run the type of offense and defense they desire. Some will choose to run the football most of the time, and others will choose to pass. But there must be a basic set of rules which keep each team from cheating in ways that they would not want any other team in the league to be able to cheat.

In the business world, if a firm can use physical threats to stop people from competing with them, if they are allowed to lie to customers about what their products contain, or they use financial sleight of hand to take advantage of customers, capitalism will never work. The government needs to be the referee that enforces these basic rules. How do I know that if I purchase a piece of land, someone stronger will not be able to take it away from me by force at some later date? Because I know the referee will step in and stop them from stealing from me in this way. How do I know that if someone has signed a contract with my firm—that if I pay upfront, they will guarantee me delivery of a certain amount of concrete on a certain day—that they will not fail to deliver but just keep my money? Because I know that the referee will throw the flag on that also. As long as the government has the power to enforce the rules, and that government can be counted on to enforce them in a uniform way, capitalism will work. And in so working, capitalism will eliminate more poverty across the globe than all the welfare and Live Aid charities ever have or ever will.

Charity is great for times of uncommon stress such as natural disasters, but only a market-based economy officiated by a consistent government has a proven track record of bring hundreds of millions of people above the poverty line and keeping them there. In so many countries today, even in democracies, the governments do not perform this refereeing function in a consistent or equitable manner. India is a sad but good example. Over the years, the government there has been spotty in enforcing the rules in a uniform way. Sometimes property rights are upheld by the courts, and sometimes not. Sometimes people who break the laws and cheat against their competitors are punished and sometimes not (often based on whether they bribed the right government official). Having a government which tells people that they cannot engage in whatever business they prefer, compete with government-owned businesses, or price products a certain way are the most likely to keep their citizens in poverty—but those with governments which are weak or inconsistent in their refereeing are only slightly better.

Allow me to use our example of football teams and referees to reinforce a few more points. What teams want is for the officials to call a fair game, and to make sure everybody plays by the rules. Therefore, there needs to be a rulebook which clearly defines what is cheating and what is not, and each team in the league must suffer the same penalty if they break a rule. What teams do not want are referees telling them how many pass plays they must attempt during the game. You may ask why the officials (or the government which they represent, in our analogy) would see it as their function to tell teams whether to pass or run the ball. Perhaps we are talking about referees at the college level, who are concerned that more people will begin to watch NFL games over college games if the college teams run the ball too much, because that is bor-ing. I can assure you the referees would end up making huge mistakes, and making the game less enjoyable compared to NFL games, if they expanded their role beyond officiating.

Government leaders make the economy less efficient and less able to eliminate poverty when they try and direct businesses into certain industries, or require them to conduct business in a certain way because they think it is better than what the coaches inside the businesses can come up with on their own. Just like many of the rules of football are designed to keep the players safe, many of the regulations of government must be designed to keep workers and consumers safe. Governments, however, often have trouble stopping at that level of intervention. Imag-ine if the referees in a football game started telling each team during the game which players they have to play and which ones they have to sit on the bench, to be "fair" to every player or "even up the competition" between the two teams. Decisions influencing the course or outcome of the game should be left to coaches and players (investors and business leaders), and the ruling authorities should just make sure everyone plays by the agreed-upon rules.

So what are some components that Christian capitalists like to see in their governments?

- A government should support contract enforcement and prop-erty rights.
- It should prevent people and companies from succeeding by cheating, bribing officials, conducting their business in a man-ner that is unsafe to employees or citizens living near the firm's operations, etc.
- It should make it easy to start a business. In so many countries today, this is a major handicap. The time it takes to get govern-ment approval to set up a business, the number of fees that have to be paid, and the number of licenses that must be obtained from different levels of government must be kept to a minimum.

- The government must stay out of trying to decide which business sectors to promote. This is part of what capitalism does best—and something at which governments all across the world have proven to be horribly ineffective. For example, over time the US Congress has pushed for the use of coal in generating electricity over the use of natural gas, which drives up the price of electricity while making pollution worse; and in promoting corn-based ethanol as a mixture in car fuel—harming our car engines, harming the environment, and making food more expensive for poor people (for an interesting summary of these and other crazy and harmful government intrusions into the energy sector of the economy, read *Power Hungry* by Robert Bryce).

The energy sector of the economy is not the only one in which the government has favored certain businesses or products over others. For decades, the government has tried to promote housing through the establishment of financial institutions called savings-and-loans (which had governmental advantages for loaning a certain percent of their capital for traditional mortgages)—which led to the savings-and-loan crisis. This was followed by the extensive funding and Congressional promotion of the government-sponsored enterprises Fannie Mae and Freddie Mac (who continued to "roll the dice," as they said on Capitol Hill on sub-prime mortgage loans)—leading to the Great Recession of 2008.

The examples here are as numerous as they are outlandish. There was a point in the 1980s where everyone thought that Japan was destined to take over the world economically because of their fast growth and the government subsidizing of key business sectors. After nearly twenty years of painfully grinding through a stagnant economy, history has taught us that one of the two main reasons their economy began to fail was that the government placed bets in the wrong area, and interfered with the financial incentives that the businessmen and women would have otherwise responded to (see the next bullet point). Today many people fear that China will ultimately dominate the world economically. I suspect, however, that fifteen years from now we will see that their threat was also short-lived because their government is overly involved in business planning and decision-making (and probably underinvolved in enforcing a common set of consistent rules). Sooner or later, as it always does, this will prove to put a significant restraint on their economic vitality.

• And finally, governments must allow businesses to fail. This may seem unchristian, but it is akin to having medicine injected into a sick child. It may seem cruel to give a crying kid a shot with a needle, but I would rather do that than have them die a slow painful death over something that could have been prevented. This is important. It is probably one of the main keys for successful capitalism. I discuss the biblical view of this economic phenomenon below. This is the second main reason that Japan started off so hot and then fell into a two-decade-long recession. They were/are very slow in allowing firms in government-supported industries to fail and in letting the banks and investors associated with those businesses suffer the consequences of those failures. When the government fully or partially runs a business or is heavily involved in regulating or financing a business, they almost never let them fail. I haven't personally seen any research on how the ratio of the number of enterprises which are opening in an economy (compared to the number which is shutting down) influences the growth, health, and poverty-reducing power of the economy over time, but it would be interesting to better understand those dynamics.

Capitalism is not perfect. There will be recessions and unemployment. There is no political and economic structure which can eliminate all declines in growth or some temporary losses of employment. Capitalism is not a perfect system; it is just (by far) the best system ever devised to cure poverty. And like a shot, the pain of the recessions is actually necessary for at least two reasons.

First, there is what economists call creative destruction—for example, buggy-makers being replaced by car-makers, typewriter repairmen being replaced by computer programmers, etc. It is unfortunate in a way, but as products improve (and our lives and health improve along with them), some industries simply become outdated, and the individuals employed in those industries are forced to move in a different direction. This does cause some short-term economic dislocation for a few, but is pivotal in allowing for much greater long-term growth and job security for everyone.

The second reason that some business failure is healthy has to do with clearing the marketplace of businesses that fail to adapt over time. Point 8 in our list from chapter 3 spoke that the Bible teaches us that we will not all be correct all of the time. In the purest forms of economic theory, it is "assumed" that each business owner will change his or her business to adapt to changes in the environment. If a mistake is made, it is uncovered and corrected. If employees are great, they get promoted; if employees are horrible, they get fired. This also means that each business-person knows the optimal price for each of their products or services, and removes unpopular products from production. But we all know that not everyone in business reacts only to economic incentives, or always reads and reacts to them in the correct way. Humans are imperfect and will not always understand the best plan of action; even when they do, they will not always undertake what makes sense or what is in their best interest. We have all seen individuals take on jobs which they could not perform, products introduced into the market which did not sell, and businesses started up in our neighborhoods which were run poorly and had to be shut down. In many of these cases, the person involved in running the business will not "admit" that mistakes were made and would just carry on making products or providing services nobody wanted, rather than admit they were wrong or change to something else. But when these firms and their managers run out of money and financing, they are forced to shut down. The government must let those businesses fade away, as they become unable to generate enough money to pay their bills.

For the most part in America, our governments do let businesses open as they desire and allow them to be closed by the market as monetary conditions dictate. Time has shown, however, that the US government will not allow the things in which *they* are involved to fail. This creates inefficiencies that grow on each other over time. Take, for example, the Social Security system. If that was just one of a number of systems you could participate in, would it be the one you would choose? Even though those in Congress do not use the system (they have their own exclusive retirement fund), they will not fix it for the rest of us. Government leaders do not want to admit their mistakes any more than private individuals; and because they can simply tax you more to pay for things even if you don't want to pay for them, they never have to admit their mistakes. If I started a tutoring business to help children learn and the children did not learn, parents would quit paying me and eventually I would have to close my doors. But if the government runs a school system and the children are not learning, they just keep right on taxing citizens, right on paying teachers, and right on not educating children with no financial incentive to force them to change.

Christians believe that we should hold government officials responsible, through our voting, for making wasteful decisions with our money, and that the government should limit their involvement to actives and services such as the military, police, courts, prisons, flood control, etc., and stay out of any businesses or sectors in the economy which private corporations can fill.

A few words about economic policy are due at this point. I have heard some urge religious leaders to call on the government to tax rich people more, so that the money can be given to poor people, because this is what churches and their leaders should be all about. The truth is, the Bible never tells us to depend on the government to help the poor—the Bible tells us to help the poor directly. It is always easier to assume that someone has more money than I do, and to vote in a politician who will take money from that person to help the poor. That way I get a feeling that I have done something moral, without really having to give up anything of mine in regard to money or time. While the government should provide a safety net for those who are in dire circumstances that are not of their own making, the Bible never says the government's role is to try and even out the wealth between the rich and poor in the country. There is an example in the Bible of a group of churches being instructed to collect money for a poor church in a different location. Care is taken to ensure to those who are giving the money that a responsible intermediary will relay the funds to their final destination, and that a witness to the transfer of the money can even be involved if it will give them greater comfort that the money is being handled responsibly. This biblical point brings out another concern with the government being involved in the "tax the rich and provide welfare for the poor" business: The US government has *not* proven to be a reliable intermediary of tax funds. They take money from the wrong people and give money to the wrong people way too often. I remember years ago reading the book *Losing Ground* by Charles Murray about how all the poverty-reduction programs in the United States implemented since the 1960s had failed so miserably. Updated research on the topic since has shown that, unfortunately, the results of those types of programs have not improved much since the '60s.

Of course, we absolutely think that those with more income should pay more taxes. The easiest way to accomplish this and still promote healthy economic growth is to provide large standard deductions which increase by family size. For example, let's suppose Family A makes $30,000 and consists of a wife, husband, and two kids, and that Family B makes $250,000 and consists of a husband, wife, and one child. If we set the family deduction at $4,000 per person and the tax rate at twenty percent for everybody, we get the following:

	Family A	Family B
Total Income	$30,000	$250,000
Deduction	$16,000	$12,000
Taxable Income	$14,000	$238,000
Tax Rate	20.00%	20.00%
Taxes Paid	$2,800	$47,600
Taxes as Percent of Total Income	9.33%	19.04%

In this example, Family B pays both a higher percent of their income in taxes (although the applied rate is twenty percent for everybody) and pay a higher dollar amount. Family B's income is about eight times greater than Family A's, but their taxes due are seventeen times greater than Family A's. In this scenario, the rich pay a greater amount in an absolute and relative sense, and yet the system is still "fair" from a biblical point of view, because everyone gets the same family deduction and pays a flat twenty-percent rate.

The current tax code is horribly unfair to almost everyone involved. Of course, all the line items in the tax code cannot be made as simple as the example above, but the framework can (and should) be made that simple. Perhaps the thing which strikes an evangelical Christian as being the most unfair about the US tax code is the deduction for mortgage interest. Why on earth would the government want to financially punish individuals who rent, in order to financially subsidize the people who own their homes? I am a homeowner so I understand that this is supposed to benefit me, but in the sense of biblical fairness this is an outrage. There are plenty of wealthy individuals who are renters but, on average, the wealth and income of those who own homes are much greater than those who rent. Having deductions in the tax code are fine—deductions for family members or charitable contributions, etc. But forcing a poor man to pay more taxes so that a rich man can get a deduction on his high-dollar mortgage is ridiculous. Those are the kinds of "unfair" policies that Christians would love to see eliminated.

The Anti-Capitalists

If poverty still exists at too high a level in this country—and is worse in almost every other country than here—and capitalism has been shown to be the best way to reduce poverty, then why do so many people not support capitalism? There are probably six main reasons:

1. *Although the more capitalistic a society is the faster poverty is reduced, no capitalistic society has ever eliminated poverty; and no capitalist claims that all poverty will ever be eliminated by a market-based system.*

Therefore, if you believe that there is some system which is "perfect" and which could tame all greed and relieve all those suffering from poverty, it would make sense to push on toward that system. The Christian does not believe that all greed can be vanquished from the earth (Matt. 18:7), and both the Old and New Testaments in the Bible teach us that poverty will never be eliminated in this world either (Deut. 15:11; John 12:3–8). Therefore, Christians are looking for the system which, in spite of its imperfections and tradeoffs, does the best job of reducing poverty. That is the system which we want our governments to support. Of course, both the Old and New Testaments also teach us that each follower of God is responsible for assisting the poor personally as well (Lev. 19:9–10; Deut. 15:7–11; Luke 3:10–11; James 2:14–17). If there is a perfect type of economic setup out there, it would be wise to keep searching for it. But if there is no perfect economic structure—and the Bible, along with all of human experience, tells us that there is not—then it makes sense to go with whichever approach is the most likely to help the greatest number of hurting people.

2. *Many people become disillusioned because they see that in a capitalistic society some people end up with a great deal more income and wealth than others.* This can be an issue for a couple of reasons. First, if we do not understand someone—if we cannot relate to them at some level—then we often hold a grudge against them and the things that are important to them. The hard-driving, creative business person is not well understood or well-liked by everybody, and so it becomes easy to become bigoted against them and the things we believe they stand for. But in this case, I am not interested, with a biblical view of the world, in being against the business person; I am interested in glorifying God by trying to help the poor. If I can only help the poor grow richer by working within a system that also allows the rich to grow richer, then so be it. My main goal is to see poverty reduced.

Related to this reason is that many of us are not happy that there are others who have more than us. Formal research has been conducted by many professors, showing that if people are given the option to have everyone's income go up—their own by $25,000 a year, and all their neighbors by $50,000 a year—a great number of people say they would choose just to let everyone stay the same instead. I have informally had this conversation with people dozens of times myself and the results are always similar. I simply ask them, "If you know you make the same as your family and friends, and could decide to give everyone a pay increase or leave everyone the same, what would you do?" Of course, they vote pay raises for everyone. But tell them they get a certain size pay increase and all their friends and family get twice that amount, and about half of them say they would leave things the same rather than make less than the others. Of course, I tell them that such a stance is not rational because they are declining an increase in income, and remind them that such a stance is also not biblical because the Bible tells me that I should rejoice when other people rejoice and not be jealous if they end up with more than me.

A final point is worth making here. Although capitalism will produce an unequal distribution of income and wealth, other systems are not better—in fact, they are much worse. Take a look at the few families which control the overwhelming portion of the wealth in communist countries such as North Korea and Cuba, or in socialist countries such as India or Venezuela. Capitalism is not perfect, but it is the best option.

3. *Many opponents point out that every successful good or service made in a capitalist economy is not necessarily the one of the best quality or the lowest price, as would be predicted by theories of economic competition, and that this drags on economic efficiency and income growth.* And I would agree with them. Years ago, the economist Thorstein Veblen wrote about such things, including in his famous book *The Theory of the Leisure Class*. He criticized what he termed "conspicuous consumption" by the wealthy, socially stuck-up business class. His point was that wealthy people will make and purchase things

just to reinforce that they are capable of consuming differentiated products and services from the masses. At the extreme, he claimed that there were some products which rich people would actually buy more of as the price went up, just because it became even more of a snob purchase as it became less affordable to regular consumers. These types of goods are today referred to as "Veblen goods." Maybe you think examples of such products in this category are the American Express card (why pay a higher annual fee for carrying a card that is accepted in fewer places than the MasterCard or Visa that all of us middle-class folks use?) or Acura automobiles.

As I type this, my sixteen-year-old Honda Civic is sitting in the garage, and it has been an outstanding car. Honda makes a good automobile. But the Acura, which is also made by Honda, seems as though it falls more into the conspicuous-consumption category. Within most product classes, there are varying qualities of goods. We have all bought something cheap which wore out too quickly and bought a similar item of better quality which lasted much longer (and therefore saved money in the long run). But within each product or service category there are almost always brand names and designer labels which are not any better than competing offerings, but which the buyer feels bestows on them some level of class or sophistication that makes them stand out from the crowd—that makes them better than the common people.

Someone suggested to me recently that the classic example of this might be Starbucks coffee. They said they enjoy a good cup of regular black coffee in the morning, and on occasion a cup of decaf black coffee after a late-night meal. In talking with other frequent coffee drinkers they knew, none of them really thought that Starbucks was anywhere near the best cup of coffee on the market. As someone else said, "There is a reason Starbucks puts all those flavors and sweeteners in their most popular-selling coffee drinks." So is it just through clever marketing to vain people that they have created a brand that gives folks the feeling of some elevated social status because of the price and prestige of their drinks? That is for you to decide.

Either way, Christians clearly see the Veblen effect as a negative for the economy, and as a downside to a free-market system. The economic theory that we learn in school says that people should purchase the best-quality products at the cheapest prices to maximize their satisfaction, but we know that this does not always happen. Even with an understanding of this issue, and clear-cut examples such as the ones given here, economic history tells us that the best way to help out the poor is for businesses to exist and operate in a free-market economy, and for the government to stay within its role as the referee of a basic set of rules.

No government in any economic structure has ever been able to do away with the leisure class and its outrageous, showy consumption. But some economic structures and government roles have proven better than others at reducing poverty. Related to this, not every wealthy person has "earned" their wealth—the original John Rockefeller and Joseph Kennedy may have been hard-working, risk-taking, job-creating businessmen in the previous century, but no one sees much value coming from the Kennedys or Rockefellers today. Do they "deserve" all that wealth they have? I do not know, but I am not worried about the rich people; I am worried about the poor people. And when governments around the world have tried to confiscate the wealth of long-time families and redistribute it to the poor, the entire country ends up worse off in just a few years. The poor actually end up worse off! It might make me look moral and feel moral to take money away from rich families who have just passed it down from one generation to the next, but God does not want me to feel moral (one of our main points from chapter 3)—He wants me to help the poor. A market-based economy helps the poor.

As a side note: If I were going to church with wealthy families such as this, I would encourage them to give to the needy—their time, their money, and their prayers. I would want them to see it as a way to worship God. I have known many people who work extra or run businesses on the side for the very purpose of having more to give away to those in need. They work harder because they see a purpose in doing so. I also know people who work less as they get into the higher tax brackets, because they see the government getting too much of their money and don't see the purpose in what they are doing with it.

4. *Many oppose capitalism out of a fear that certain large businesses would ultimately be able to take over the economy and dominate the political scene, leaving the rest of us in subjection to them.* Again, a survey of recent economic history shows this is not a realistic fear. The companies which were mentioned in newspaper editorials and economic books as being the biggest threat of achieving this dominance—firms such as Standard Oil, US Steel, General Motors, Great Northern Railroad—not only did not take over, but in many cases do not even exist any longer. I had a conversation with an old college buddy some years back and he mentioned he thought this was still a threat with what he called near monopoly companies at the time such as CitiBank, Walmart, and Microsoft. More than a decade having passed since that conversation, I am not sure that anyone sees a threat of domination coming from any of those companies. They still exist but they do not dominate in any sense of the word. No single company or group of companies will ever be able to do that in a capitalist society.

5. *As silly as it may sound, some people are opposed to capitalism because the entrepreneurs who start and run business are not like them.* It is a natural instinct for people to be cautious, or even biased, against those who are different (point 15 in chapter 3). We not only have a tendency to look at those who are different with a negative slant, but we also tend to see those who are different as all being like one another, which we also see as bad. It is all too easy to slip into thinking that all businesspeople are different from you and that none of them share the same personality, character traits, or aspirations as you. The distrust of them as individual people then easily transfers over to a dislike of their line of work, etc.

As I walked the halls of economics departments at major universities, I was amazed at how biased the well-educated professors were against businessmen and women simply because those entrepreneurs were different from them. I was equally amazed that they were more biased against those who had worked their way up from poverty or more humble economic and social beginnings than they were against the rich kids who had inherited their family's businesses. During the 2012 presidential election cycle, a relatively well-known economist actually wrote an op-ed piece claiming that Mitt Romney should not be president because he was a businessman. I should note that, while it is not as prevalent (or harmful), many young entrepreneurs I have worked with are also disparaging of academic and government economists for no other reason than they are different from them, and it creates natural misunderstanding and distrust between them.

6. *Point 19 in chapter 3 discussed the fact that many people have a need to attain at least the appearance of a certain moral standing, either to satisfy their ideal image of themselves or in an attempt to compensate for what they feel are unmoral activities in other areas of their lives.* Some initiatives which seem to impart a feeling of moral standing, such as environmental issues or being anti-war, may ebb and flow over time, but one of the most constant themes is being anti-capitalism. This is not to be confused with jealousy. It is amazing how many multimillionaire entertainers and politicians (who have more money than the businessmen and women they are complaining about) try to outdo themselves in how vocal they can be in criticizing capitalism.

Before we leave this chapter on economics, it is probably a good idea to discuss a particular proverb:

> Two things I ask of you; deny them not to me before I die: Remove far from me falsehood and lying; give me neither poverty nor riches; feed me with the food that is needful for me, lest I be full and deny you and say, "Who is the LORD?" or lest I be poor and steal and profane the name of my God (Prov. 30:7–9).

Here, the biblical writer is asking God to keep them from being either too poor or too rich in this life, because both increase the risk of sinning. Just as I love food and approve of everyone having enough to keep themselves and their families full and healthy, but do not want to see people eat in an addicted or unhealthy way, I approve of people working hard at their jobs and learning to become more productive in them over time (as the Bible commands us to do both) and approve of capitalism (because it is the best system for creating the most jobs and the most income for the most people)—but I do not recommend to any given person that they dedicate themselves only to getting wealthy, as this becomes as unhealthy as any other obsession or addiction. I would never want my children or nieces and nephews to go hungry or without basic medical treatment due to poverty, but I also do not wish that they win the lottery or become an American Idol.

CHAPTER 6

The View of Science

Are science and religion at odds with each other?

a. Yes
b. No

The answer is "b," no.

The Bible and Science: The Perfect Marriage

Of all the misconceptions about Bible-believing religious folks, perhaps the craziest one is that we are opposed to science because for some reason science and religion can't mix. Even the most elementary students of science or history know that some of the most famous and relevant scientists—Isaac Newton, Lord Kelvin, James Maxwell, and Johannes Kepler, for example—were Christians who saw themselves as exploring and documenting God's creation, as they felt biblically mandated to do. Some of the earliest work done in the field of genetics was formulated and completed by a Christian believer, Gregor Mendel. The man called the father of the scientific method, Francis Bacon, wrote that he understood how an initial brush with science might lead one to believe they were going to end up not believing as deeply in religion, but what he actually found was that the deeper you get into science, the greater your faith will become.

The idea that science and religion are not compatible is perpetuated by a minority of individuals within the scientific community. Evangelicals, though, have never had a problem with science, and would never think that science and religion are not compatible. The aforementioned father of the physics of quantum mechanics, Max Planck, stated in his book *Where Is Science Going:* "There can never be any real opposition between religion and science; for the one is the complement of the other." In fact, scientific and medical discoveries are of great benefit to mankind, and continue to reveal to men just how incredibly awesome God and His creation are. Those with a biblical worldview are huge fans of science and eagerly support, participate in, and follow ongoing scientific discovery.

Before we move on to the heart of the chapter, digress with me for a moment back to the Christmas stories told in the gospels of Matthew and Luke. As a young person, I remember being taught that there were multiple lessons to be taken from how the realization of Jesus' birth occurred. From Luke 2, we are taught that for the Jewish people—the religious people of the day who sought after God—God's revelation was direct, though the revelation was to shepherds who held the lowest rung on the social ladder in those days. The point was: For those brought up in a Jewish or Christian religious tradition, God would reveal His plan of salvation directly to us—as it turned out, through the Bible—and that even the most common person would have God's information available directly to them. They did not have to rely on sophisticated religious leaders to work on their behalf.

But what about those who are not raised in a family that uses the Bible? What about people who pride themselves on the use of their logic more than their faith? That is where the story of the wise men from Matthew 2 comes in. These individuals were not Jews raised with the Old Testament Scriptures. They were educated people from a different race and culture. They would have been the forerunners to today's university-educated astrophysicists or cosmologists. They studied the stars and attempted to identify and plot the motions of planets. They came to a knowledge and interest of Jesus-related things by studying the natural, physical world around them. Their journey was much longer and more complicated than that of the shepherds—notice the shepherds were there on the night Jesus was born in a stable, and the wise men did not show up until Jesus' family had found a house to stay in the days, weeks, or maybe months later—but it was their wisdom, curiosity, and studies that brought them the same knowledge as the Jews had received more directly.

The apostle Paul wrote, "For what can be known about God is plain to them, because God has shown it to them. For his invisible attributes, namely, his eternal power and divine nature, have been clearly perceived, ever since the creation of the world, in the things that have been made. So they are without excuse" (Rom. 1:19–20). With these lessons in mind, as I was growing up and attending school and college, I always saw science as a study that complimented my faith. Of course, some findings have challenged the opinions that some of us have held from time to time, but science was never seen as a threat or a competitor. Science and the rigorous application of the scientific method is seen by Christians as a way to better understand the truth—as a way to continue to reveal how awesome, complex, and creative God is.

In a world where we have so much technology at our fingertips, it can become all too easy for even the most faithful Christian to begin to not have the appropriate awe and wonder for God Almighty. But as science continues to uncover and reveal the majesty of the universe we live in, it still serves as an avenue to draw logical intellectuals to faith, and to remind faithful people of all the wonderfully complex characteristics that have been documented about the world in which we live.

The best-known example of a prominent atheist intellectual coming to believe in God through the evidence of science would have to be Anthony Flew. As a philosophy professor at Oxford University, Flew was considered to be the most eloquent spokesman for atheism. He wrote papers defending what he considered to be the logical tenets of atheism, and participated in ongoing debates about the subject. When Flew changed his mind to a definite belief in a god of some sort—the journey of which is covered in his book *There Is a God: How the World's Most Notorious Atheist Changed His Mind*—he said his new belief was based purely on the latest scientific evidence. For an example of how scientific discoveries continue to point to the awesome complexities of God, read through Michael Denton's book *Nature's Destiny*.

The Intellectual Corruption of Power and Adoration

By now, some of you are probably thinking about the dispute between Galileo and the leaders of the Catholic Church. Did this incident, you wonder, show that science and the Bible are at odds? Not at all. Actually, it is just one more historical episode confirming the biblical worldview. In the days of Copernicus and Galileo, the leading authorities in the Catholic Church were power-hungry and out of control, trying to play roles far beyond anything the Bible assigned to them. The leaders of the Catholic Church wanted to build and maintain political and economic power all throughout Europe. They wanted to dictate what people were exposed to, in order to try and control what they would believe—and therefore, who they would hold in esteem as their earthly masters. There was absolutely no biblical basis for their overreach, just egotism and a hunger for power. Ultimately, other religious leaders such as Martin Luther opposed the Catholic leaders for exactly these reasons, and sought to bring the church's focus and its use of the Bible back to their proper places.

As early scientists began to plot the motion of the planets and search the stars through telescopes, they came to realize that the sun was the center of our solar system and that the earth revolved around it. So why did a select group of religious leaders oppose these findings? Because they felt they were unbiblical? No. Because that group of religious leaders had carefully developed and protected an unbelievably powerful standing in the world and the lives of all the people around them, and did not want that position threatened. Religious individuals and religious leaders are just as susceptible to their pride and the intoxication of having power and control over others as anyone else. They saw these scientific intellectuals as the biggest threat to what they perceived as their own supremacy. It seemed very possible to the cardinals and the Pope that people might begin to look on these scientists for direction in certain areas of their lives, and that government officials might consult with them as well and they lashed out in frustration.

The Bible never says that the earth is at the center of the universe, galaxy, or solar system. But if those religious leaders were discredited by the proof of science all those years ago, why is there still a supposed conflict between science and religion today? Because the shoe has flipped to the other foot. Today there are a number of intellectuals (many scientists prominent among them) who feel as though all common men should admire them, look to them for knowledge, and take their direction from them. These individuals have the same struggles with pride and desire to influence other people's lives as some religious leaders did centuries ago.

The issue is not whether religious men are opposed to science, or whether scientific men are opposed to religion; it is simply one of people in either field gaining a certain level of respect and influence which then makes them hungry for more. In these cases, the individuals use whatever public or political influence they can muster to press ahead and increase their sway and feed their egos. Scientists have had good laughs over time when they demonstrate the natural causes of items such as thunder or disease, which nonbiblical religions used to assign to mysterious forces or spirits. But I am not defending any of those silly, manmade religions. I am simply saying that the Bible tells us we should engage in scientific endeavors, and that science has never proven anything in the Bible wrong.

Of course, we see many scientists who are known (or even popular) in the public sphere trying to strongly argue that science and biblical Christianity are not compatible. The main reason is because religion competes with them for influence and prestige in the world. If you believe God created not just everything else but also created you, and you believe that Jesus died to save you, it literally shapes how you think about the world. If these well-known men of science want to be the only ones who shape what you think about the world (based, of course, on their brilliance), they must first convince you not to take religion seriously. When the overwhelming majority of people continue to place religious thought and beliefs in high esteem, the scientists get angry and combative (as the Catholic head honchos did centuries ago). But as their attacks become more political and more personal, and as they desperately seek to gather allies and redefine the terms of the debate, they lose credibility at an increasing rate.

In survey after survey, the majority of people still say that they believe in God and in heaven. Most also continue to report that they believe God played a heavy role in what was created, and that they still have lingering doubts about all the evolutionary claims made by science relative to biological life and its diversity. Obviously this fans the flames of the scientists' anger, causing them to become even more hardened in their positions.

Why do people (not just Christians) continue to believe so much in the need for God and His creative capabilities? There are two intertwined reasons:

1. We understand that science has made incredible progress over the last few centuries, and yet what we think we understood about life, whence it came, and how it changes has not progressed compared to what scientists have promised us was going to happen. So many of these scientific predictions about recreating life and developing a Grand Unification Theory (the theory of everything) came with an unnecessary defiance, and the implied target seems to be the breaking down of God Himself rather than the advancement of scientific knowledge. Their credibility has (rightly) come under review, as these predictions fail.

2. Just as Francis Bacon predicted, the initial discoveries in the fields of biology and physics seemed to be building a coffin for religion, but further discoveries seem to point unquestionably to some supernatural force—something outside the ability for natural, scientific laws to explain—being necessary to explain what exists and where it came from.

The Point of No Darwinian Return

The Catholic leaders I have been critical of above got ahead of themselves over the issue of whether the sun or the earth was moving, and made that argument their point of no return. I think atheist scientists did that with Darwin's book *On the Origin of Species*. From the publication of that work (which was creative and brilliant in its context), some overreaching scientists put their stake in the ground and declared that science was on the path to explaining away God. More than 150 years later, they have determined that it is too late to give up on the cause, even though the hypothesis has essentially failed. The result is that as predictions miss their mark and hypotheses fail to be validated through repeated experiments, these scientists become more entrenched and make even more extreme claims of things to come (and sadly, resort to old-fashioned name calling and intellectual bullying in a number of cases). Obviously, as predictions about what science will explain, and how, grow bolder and at a faster rate and are promised over shorter time-frames (and people get tired of being called names), the general pub-lic—including but not limited to Christians—becomes more skeptical.

When Darwin published his book on the theory of evolution (which, as we will discuss in greater detail in a moment, did not theo-rize about how the earth got here), he did make a simple guess about how life could have begun on earth (his infamous "primordial soup"). Soon, other scientists were leading the public to believe that the issue of how life began would soon be solved. Darwin himself assumed that the archeological record would sooner rather than later support his theory of evolution with massive fossil evidence. To date, the fossil evidence is close to nonexistent—there isn't a single "missing link"; there are liter-ally billions of missing links. And the idea of the primordial soup as the origin of biological life has essentially been discarded (for literature on these two topics, see Michael Denton's book *Evolution: A Theory in Crisis* and Paul Davies' book *The 5th Miracle*, respectively).

In the 1950s, scientists really began to think that they would soon be able to establish (and recreate) the cause of life on earth. But again they failed—and actually pretty miserably, as those experiments ended with just a few amino acids floating in a goopy liquid. In the introduc-tion to Stephen Hawking's book *A Brief History of Time* (first published in 1988), Carl Sagan wrote "This book is also a book about God . . . or perhaps the absence of God." Sagan closed out his introduction to the book saying that if the ideas science was working on at the moment came to fruition, there would be "nothing for a Creator to do."[8] Later on in the book, Hawking himself wrote, "so long as the universe had a beginning, we could suppose it had a creator. But if the universe is really completely self-contained, having no boundary or edge, it would have neither beginning nor end; it would simply be. What place then for a creator?"[9]

Scientists today, however, understand that the universe did have a beginning and will have an end—at least as far as order, usable energy, and biological life are concerned. Not only has science not proven that a god is not necessary; it *has* proven the need for some creative, energetic force hitherto unexplained by scientific laws. For a more detailed counterpoint on these topics, read John Lennox's recent book *God's Undertaker: Has Science Buried God?*

Am I saying that the general public and/or Christians today are a bit leery of some of the overreaching claims of certain practitioners in science? Yes! But isn't this lack of trust irrational given the brilliance of scientific discoveries and the progress that the scientific community has made over time? No. In fact, the nonscientific public suffers from the "once bitten, twice shy" syndrome, which derives from just the opposite set of circumstances. Let me explain.

Some anti-religion proponents of science have claimed that as scientific abilities and knowledge increase from point A to point B, as Carl Sagan wrote, there will no longer be a role for God. Through either outright claims or strong implications, the anti-God scientific crowd has led us to believe over the past century or more that science could and soon would explain where all matter came from, how some of it came to life, how those life forms changed, etc. But scientific abilities and knowledge moved from point A through the level of point B and on to points C and D without those questions being answered. In fact,

[8] Carl Sagan, Introduction to *A Brief History of Time* by Stephen Hawking (New York: Bantam Books, 1988), x.
[9] Stephen Hawking, *A Brief History of Time* (New York: Bantam Books, 1988), 140–141.

as science has progressed more unknowns related to those issues have arisen than questions answered.

I remember the conversations I had with colleagues in 1996 when the news of Dolly the cloned sheep hit the newspapers. What an outstanding and fascinating scientific advancement. As I understand it, the DNA from one sheep was implanted to replace the genetic material in an egg from another sheep, and that modified embryo was carried and delivered by a third sheep. As we marveled at the event, we discussed what we thought the implications were for science and religion. Specifically, what track was science on, what was next, and did cloning a sheep amount to science trying to "play God"? We (about two-thirds of us Christians of one variety or another) saw that, even though science was making remarkable leaps in how life worked and was mastering how to manipulate existing biological entities in impressive and progressive ways, they had no greater idea how life started (and less confidence in their ability to replicate it anytime soon) than they had before the cloning happened. We agreed that they were not playing God as long as human DNA and embryos were not involved, because humans are more than just physical beings.

Every high school student has to learn about the DNA helix and how cells replicate themselves through a tricky little process of unraveling and reconnecting the "rungs" on the DNA ladder. And it is explained to us in those classes how complicated this genetic code is even for the simplest of organisms, such as bacteria. As researchers began to map these genomes, it was obvious that science was continuing on at its blistering pace. And then just a couple of years ago, scientists created a "synthetic cell." This is a perfect example of what I describe as both the abilities of science (the tools that they have to work with, for example) and the knowledge of science (developing a deeper and more accurate understanding of the world we live in) increasing in tandem to allow for amazing progress. As J. Craig Venter and Daniel Gibson wrote in *The Wall Street Journal*, "the process of synthesizing a cell began at a computer." They go on to say "we refer to the cell we have created as being a synthetic cell because it is controlled by a synthetic genome assembled from chemically synthesized pieces of DNA." What? So these guys derived a new cell with a new set of operating instructions that did not exist before. I say new because in their words, the "resulting cells will not contain any molecules that were present in the original recipient cells." Let me quote for you one of the benefits they note that human-kind will likely derive from the use of this procedure. "We already have funding from the National Institutes of Health to use our synthetic DNA tools to build synthetic segments of every known flu virus so that we can rapidly build new vaccine candidates in less than 24 hours."[10]

Have you or anyone you know ever gotten a flu shot, only to come down with the flu a few weeks later? That happens because the flu virus changes its genetic structure rapidly (and in a strange way). When it comes time each year to develop a flu vaccine, medical researchers essentially make an educated guess about what strand of flu will be most prevalent in the coming year, and it is that strand of dead flu virus that is injected into everyone in the fall of the year so that our bodies can develop a defense against it. But if the actual strand of flu virus that attacks your body is different from the strand or strands with which you were inoculated, your body doesn't have the head start in defending itself that you thought it would when you received the vaccine. These gentlemen are saying they may be able to help the medical establishment drastically reduce response time to creating a vaccine in reaction to an epidemic occurring "on the ground."

There are other cool examples from science and medicine about how advanced our working knowledge of biological life has become. We have all read the stories of a baboon heart being implanted into a human, or of mechanical hearts being implanted. From just the examples of Dolly and synthetic bacteria cells, however, we can see that science can manipulate biological life in every conceivable way. Creatures can be cloned, and genetic information can be taken from a source cell of one type, adjusted using computers and lab chemicals, then reimplanted into a

---

[10] J. Craig Venter and Daniel Gibson, "How We Created the First Synthetic Cell," *The Wall Street Journal*, May 26, 2010.

destination cell of a different type. This is incredibly complex work. We understand so much about how life functions, and have been brilliant enough to develop the tools to work at the level of genetic code that we can literally change, recreate, and newly create millions of things.

But before I leave the subject, allow me one more quote from the article by Venter and Gibson. In discussing how their work was in many ways an extension of work that had been completed decades earlier by Arthur Kornberg, they say, "Kornberg did not create life in a test tube, nor did we create life from scratch. We transformed existing life into new life."[11]

There was a point just a few decades ago where certain scientists were propagating the view that they would be able to create life from scratch. After all, if it had just randomly popped up on earth without any intelligent direction in an atmosphere simpler than what we live in now, how hard could it be for brilliant scientists to make it happen on purpose in a controlled laboratory? There was not a thought yet that we would be able to manipulate DNA to the point of cloning animals or making synthetic cells, but perhaps once we could make life in a test tube, science would be able to progress to do those other, more glamorous things. The reality is that science has moved past the level that was expected, into unseen realms of capability and comprehension. But along this scientific journey we have come to realize that while we understand much more about life and how it functions than we thought possible we actually know less than we thought—nothing, in fact—about how it began.

In *The 5th Miracle*, Paul Davies writes about science's journey to understand the transition from dead material to living organisms, and directly answers the ultimate question in his book: "Can the laws of nature as we presently comprehend them account for such a transition? I do not believe they can. To see why not it is necessary to dig a bit deeper into the informational character of life."[12] No one, regardless of their genius, can explain using the laws of nature (the common term that

---

[11] Ibid.
[12] Paul Davies, *The 5th Miracle* (*New York*: Simon & Schuster Paperbacks, 1999), 115.

Davies uses for scientific law) how dead material—dirt, metal, water or minerals—came to life (and in such a way that it could reproduce itself before dying). If there is no natural explanation for biological life, then maybe, the explanation is supernatural?

In fact, Francis Crick, the Nobel Prize-winning scientist who co-discovered the makeup of DNA, while acknowledging that natural, scientific laws could not explain how life came to be on earth, put forth an idea that life must have been dropped off here sometime in the distant past by beings that must have been quite intelligent and creative and powerful (though we have not been able to detect them with modern scientific instruments). He called his idea "directed panspermia." I don't have a Nobel Prize—and seems to be no great threat that I will be awarded one anytime soon—but I think I can summarize directed panspermia: Something powerful, creative, and intelligent, which exists outside man's ability to scientifically detect, had to intentionally put life on earth, because it is not scientifically possible for life to spontaneously have created itself on earth. And one of the ways that you could describe God would be: Something powerful, creative, and intelligent, which exists outside man's ability to detect scientifically, intentionally put life on earth, because it is not possible for life to spontaneously have created itself on earth.

The problem for science is this: If life could have spontaneously erupted on earth at some point, science now has the knowledge, tools, and ability to recreate life in that way. It can't recreate life, however, because it did not simply spontaneously come into existence by some random natural process.

But Before Biological Life and Evolution . . .

Of course, we are way ahead of ourselves here in determining that the current state of knowledge suggests that life could not have spontaneously developed on earth. Before matter can come to life, there has to be matter to begin with. The first question science has to answer, if they are going to replace God, is: From whence came all the material stuff that exists in the universe?

The laws of nature tell us very, very plainly that small amounts of matter don't just pop into existence, so trying to believe that trillions of tons of matter just popped into existence is foolishness. One way that scientists tried for decades to get around this problem was to say that somehow matter has just always been there, making it technically outside the realm of what science could study with natural, scientific laws. But, as stated, no one believes today that the universe is eternal. The Bible says that "in the beginning, God created. . . ." Science is right! Stuff has not always existed. God has always existed—the Bible describes God as "from everlasting to everlasting" (Ps. 103:17). But material matter, according to the Bible, had a definite starting point (the beginning), and a definite starting cause or catalyst (God the creator). So if the scientific community at least agrees with the Bible that the universe did not always exist but in fact had a beginning, we are back to our question: From whence came all the material stuff that exists in the universe?

The latest ploy by certain atheists within the scientific community is to try and concoct ways for explaining how matter (and probably biological life) just appeared at some point in time without having to have always existed or having to be created by a willful force. The problem with this approach, which includes entrants such as multiverse theory, is that they cannot be tested by science because *they* are supernatural—outside the natural laws of our universe. The other problem is that they don't make much sense.

John Horgan, who authored the book *The End of Science*, wrote in the review of another book, "I'm not a fan of 'multiverse' theories, which I think of as science fiction with equations."[13] That sounds about right. The problem here is that many of these multiverse theories move outside of what is possible in our universe, within the natural laws that science itself has uncovered. For example, multiverse theories say that our universe (which came into existence at a point in time) perhaps came from another universe which has existed forever and operates

[13] John Horgan, "To Err Is Progress," review of *The Beginning of Infinity* by David Deutsch, *The Wall Street Journal*, July 20, 2011.

under different scientific laws. In other words, in order to explain the origin of our world, even atheist PhDs have to resort to going to something that has always existed and that is supernatural—something that resides outside the scope and control of the laws that direct the world we live in. That supernatural something which can flaunt the laws of nature sounds a lot like God, doesn't it?

In his well-written, educational book entitled *Who Made God?*, Edgar Andrews responds to another scientist who has written about multiverse theories, Victor Stenger. Andrews says, "The fact is that neither Dr. Stenger nor anyone else has a clue—exact or inexact—about how the universe might have originated by material causes. . . . Furthermore, to invoke an invisible, inaccessible, eternal and totally unknowable prior universe as the material cause of the one we know, can hardly be dignified as a 'scientific' account of origins."[14] It is no wonder that the scientists who use these outrageous and untestable theories lose credibility with the general public. Nor is it surprising that when they feel they are losing the attention and admiration of the public, they point at Christians and scream at us even louder. Creating an enemy (especially one that can be blamed for holding up progress) is the fastest, and maybe only way for a falling star to halt its decline.

There are other outstanding issues which cause us to question the degree to which science can explain everything without resorting to supernatural explanations, such as the incredibly low state of entropy in the universe, which all the natural laws tell us required a great deal of energy to have been intentionally directed to that purpose at the beginning of time. Of course, that leads to the question: From whence came that tremendous amount of energy before anything natural existed, and how did it get so directed? Digging into all those details is beyond the scope of this book, so again I eagerly direct you to the lively discussions you will find on such topics in Dr. Andrews' aforementioned *Who Made God?*

Philosophers have written about the impossibility of inorganic matter (water, iron ore, etc.) developing consciousness over time—no

---

[14] Edgar Andrews, *Who Made God?* (Carlisle, PA: EP Books USA, 2009), 102–121.

matter how long a time period you allow. Even complex items intentionally designed by brilliant creators (airplanes and space stations) cannot ever be imagined developing an awareness of themselves or the ability to "think" outside of how they are programmed. There is simply no natural, scientific way for matter to gain the awareness or consciousness that defines human life. And though this is true, there is really a more fundamental argument related to creation and the Creator.

The Headline Read "The Greatest Discovery Ever Made"

Suppose the headline in the newspapers read "The Greatest Discovery Ever Made: Complex Industrial-Like Facility Discovered on Distant Planet." The article went on to describe this massive layout which was fully self-sustaining. One portion functioned as a factory, ran by self-adjusting computers, which produced and installed spare parts for all the other buildings, machines, and robots in the complex. Another area produced fuel from raw inputs—which were grown in still another area—which robots regularly injected into vehicles resembling locomotives, which moved components from one end of the complex to another. The article closed by noting that there was no life found on the planet, intelligent or otherwise.

If a story such as this broke, there is absolutely no doubt that one hundred percent of the scientists alive throughout all the history of the world would have unequivocally stated that some form of intelligent life was responsible for intentionally engineering and producing this complex system. Though some scientists and other researchers would begin trying to decipher how the mechanics of the system worked, most would be much more interested in figuring out who put the facility there in the first place. Governments and grant foundations around the world would pour billions of dollars into looking for the intelligent life that *must* exist to have put such an extravagant, interdependent system in place.

Now suppose someone proposed that there need not be an intelligent creator at all. Their hypothesis was that all of what was discovered was probably created by random forces—sandstorms, lighting flashes, floods, strong winds, etc. We all know that such a notion would be immediately dismissed, and that the search for the intelligent architect and engineer would continue unabated. If the person pressed his or her hypothesis harder, they would be ridiculed and told that nothing approaching the mechanical complexity and synergistic functions of this massive factor had ever been produced by random forces on earth or anywhere else in the universe. If the antagonist continued by arguing that this system could have come into existence with no intelligent designer because it had built-in ways to self-sustain and self-replicate itself, the world's scientists would have this person committed. They would (likely very impolitely) tell the person that the very fact that the system was self-replicating proves beyond any doubt that it must have had a creator. "If what we see are computers driven by software that is coded to have them manufacture other computers, we understand where each additional computer comes from," they would say. "But where, then, did the first computer come from, if there was no existing computer coded with that software to make it? Logic, not to mention common sense, is altogether against your 'it just popped into existence' theory," they would shout.

Now, let's assume that a few months later a discovery is made on another planet in the same galaxy. What is discovered is also self-contained and self-sustaining but is much more complex—thousands of times more complex than the expertly crafted factory previously brought to light. Again, common sense, logic, and the laws of science would all dictate that there must be a creator involved here as well. And all the scientists and philosophers would agree, eagerly devoting attention to the search for so grand an architect and engineer.

But, if this more complex, synergistic system contained self-replicating biological entities, thousands of scientists would immediately make claims—contrary to common sense, their own intrinsic beliefs, scientific knowledge, and the rules of logic—against the need for, or likelihood of, a creator. If the term "hardware" in the first discovery is replaced with the word "cell," and the term "software" from the first discovery is replaced by the phrase "genetic code," then rational scientists would become irrational hypocrites, throwing their own logic out the window and (ineffectively) arguing against the need for a creator.

In addition to the fact that natural laws fail miserably to account for what we see in existence today, it is this self-contained, synergistic nature, self-replicating biological entities in our universe, and the planet we call home that makes the Nobel Prize-winners and the devoted, life-long atheists such as Francis Crick and Anthony Flew (just to name a few famous names out of thousands) claim that some intelligent, creative force exists somewhere and is responsible for what we see and who we are. Say what you want about the logical, analytical people who are determined to follow the evidence where it leads regardless of the outcome (such as Dr. Flew, a believer in a creator god who was a deist, or myself a believer in a creator God and Bible-believing Christian), but at least we are not logically inconsistent at best or flat-out hypocrites at worst. We would react the same way to either newspaper headline discussed above. If you would not, then you have to honestly ask yourself what preconceived beliefs you are bringing into your study of the evidence.

So Where Are We At?

It is necessary to reemphasize that as much scientific progress as has been made over just the last century, the more we learn the more we realize that we have discovered and/or explained much less of the universe than we thought. We thought we were one hundred miles away from some grand unification theory which explains everything, yet we have marched five hundred miles forward—only to discover that we are now, *at least*, ten thousand miles away from even a rudimentary grand unification theory. The progress and discoveries in those five hundred miles have been astounding in an absolute sense (i.e., what we know that we did not know before), but humbling in a relative sense (what we realize we don't know compared to what we once thought we didn't know).

For example, some fascinating research (which originally was trying to determine if the universe was static or expanding—and if expanding was it doing so at a slowing, steady, or increasing rate) has shown in just the last few decades that all the matter and energy we thought made up the universe is actually around only 4.5 percent of the total, with the rest being made up of mysterious "dark matter" and "dark energy." One of the most readable accounts I have encountered on this topic is Richard Panek's book *The 4 Percent Universe*.

It is popular in scientific, philosophical, and religious circles to discuss not just the "whats" of our universe and our existence in it but the "whys" as well. At a treetop level, I break down in the illustration below what I see as the eight major questions that need to be resolved before science can make God irrelevant.

EXPLAIN WHERE matter / energy came from	DEFINE WHAT matter / energy exists and what its properties are	EXPLAIN WHY the rules governing nature are what they are	DEFINE WHAT rules & natural laws govern the universe	EXPLAIN WHY & HOW some matter came to life	DEFINE WHAT organic life is and how biological systems function	EXPLAIN WHY there is such biological diversity	DEFINE WHAT living things do to adapt (and survive) over time

These are the main issues which science endeavors to understand and explain. I have placed them together in categories (the where of matter with the what of matter, the where and whats of biological life side by side, etc.), while also trying to put them in some rough order of importance from right to left. The most pressing question is: Where did all the material stuff in the universe/world come from? It should be noted that modern science has really only made progress on the "what" type questions. Though I have marveled throughout the pages of this chapter at the accomplishments of science—and they are impressive in scope and number—if we rearrange the chart a little bit and take account of the fact that we have only been analyzing 4.5 percent of what exists in the universe, it becomes plain that science is much more limited than the pride of some scientists will allow them to admit.

Science has answered virtually no questions on the left-hand side of the chart above and now realizes that for some of the questions which have been answered on the right-hand side of the divide, it has covered only 4.5 percent of all the stuff that exists. And what we know about

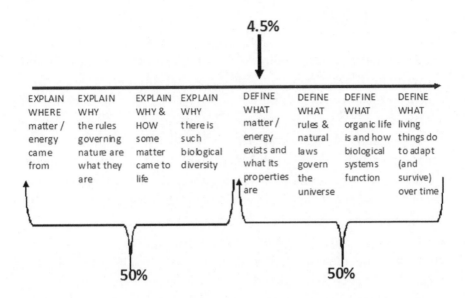

that 4.5 percent is far from complete. For example, physicists are looking for that grand unifying theory which meshes what we understand about macrophysics (general relativity/gravity) and microphysics (quantum mechanics). As of now, what seems to be true about the laws of large things (the movement of planets) doesn't mesh with what seems to be true about the rules governing super-small things (activities at the subatomic level). This is a major gap in modern science.

Of course, we don't hear a lot about science trying to explain where matter came from or what natural, scientific laws would have to be suspended in order for us to see the world as we actually do see it. That ugly part of science generally stays hidden from public view. What we hear about over and over is evolution. That is the theory which atheists have decided to cling to (which, in hindsight, has not turned out to be a great idea). So where does evolution fit into my illustrations?

First, let me ask another question: Do evangelical Christians believe in the scientific theory of the survival of the fittest (a concept which comes from Darwinian evolution)? The answer is yes, we absolutely do! Why is it that some species of birds have survived across changing climates and environments, while others have become extinct? One main reason is because as things have changed, some representatives within a species are better adapted for the new environment, and usually take over at some point. Those most fit for the new environment are the ones which survive in it.

Assume that at some point back in time cheetahs were larger and slower than they are now, but that a few cheetah offspring were born much skinnier with longer legs and a longer tail (which is needed as a stabilizer at fast speeds). On a portion of the African plains with no larger predators, the fat, slow cheetahs would always dominate. But if other larger and more powerful predators moved in which competed for the slower prey animals that the big cheetahs went after, they might begin to starve to death. The cheetahs which just happened to be born skinny and fast could survive, however, by going after faster prey that the bigger competitors could not catch. At some point, a majority of the cheetahs on the plain (or perhaps all of them) would be the skinny fast type, because they were the most fit to survive in a new environment where there was a lot of competition for slow prey but none for fast prey. Every species has great diversity built into it. Think about humans, all the races, and all the different types of body builds and abilities.

Other species show even greater diversity. There are hundreds of types of domesticated dogs and cats. The idea of the survival of the fittest makes perfect sense, and documented cases have been established in science where the interplay of this natural diversity and the changing strains of the environments in which living things exist have caused everything from antibiotic-resistant bacteria to the fastest cheetahs and the giraffes with the longest necks to survive. Evangelical Christians see survival of the fittest taking its place in the far right of the illustration below.

Where those with a biblical worldview disagree with the overly aggressive (and overly optimistic) claims of some in science is whether evolution involves more than just the survival of the fittest within a species over time, but also somehow includes the mutation of one kind of animal into another type of animal.

Of course, all that is needed to take the question marks off the graphic above is for science to be able to replicate one type of species evolving into another. I do not mean one type of small bird that has lived isolated for so long that it can no longer breed with other types of

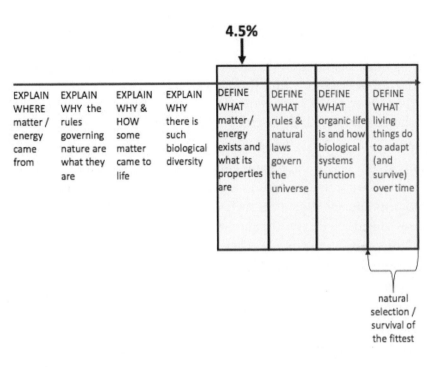

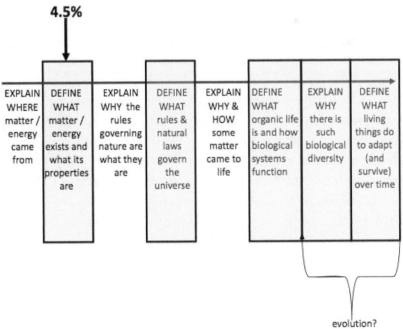

birds, or a strain of bacteria becoming resistant to a certain antibiotic but remaining very much bacteria—I mean birds changing into something other than birds, or bacteria changing into something other than bacteria, maybe into a fruit fly or a worm.

Science's Dirty Little Secret

And here is where we bump into the box that contains science's dirty little secret. One subpopulation of the scientific community has forced mutations into the genes and bred millions and millions of generations of fast-producing organisms such as E. coli and fruit flies trying to produce something other than another E. coli or a fruit fly in the process. Of course, they have utterly failed to do this! The truth is, scientists now know that they cannot do this. As discussed in the opening of the book, the validation of some scientific theories cannot be made by simply observing nature. Scientists have to formulate some tenets into testable hypotheses and intentionally seek to prove or disprove them through designed experiments in a laboratory. The search for the Higgs-Boson is one example of this type of experiment, and one "kind" of animal evolving into a different "kind" of animal through genetic mutation is another example. But scientists know how to test whether this theory is valid or not, and have designed and carried out those tests in well-controlled laboratory experiments. It is not that science has yet to figure out how to test the hypothesis, or that more work needs to be done to determine whether the hypothesis is true. The exact experiments needed have been designed and executed and the results are conclusive and clear—one type of plant or animal *cannot* evolve or turn into another type of plant or animal. It is not that it occurs too rarely in nature to be an effective engine for Darwinian evolution; it is that it does not occur at all, because scientifically it *cannot* occur at all. That is what scientists have proven in their own laboratories.

Of course, the Bible stated long ago that God created specific plant and animal types to only be able to breed within "their kind" (Gen. 1:21, 24–25). House cats and zebras cannot mate and produce viable offspring, and no matter how many cats we breed one of them is not going to give birth to a zebra.

We can think this way about the scientific studies that have been completed involving the theory of evolution at the genetic level. Imagine there is a machine (the biological entity) designed for a specific function (for example, spot welding components on an assembly line in a factory) that is driven exclusively by very complicated software (its DNA). Scientists are interested in understanding whether or not it is possible for this specific machine to be changed by its own software (to evolve, if you will) into a drone that flies around and delivers packages. Their first approach is to bombard the machine's software with x-rays and see if the code would "naturally" mutate into a set of instructions that changed and operated the machine as a drone (this would be akin to scientists observing processes in nature). Seeing that this process was not producing any positive change in the machine and its operations (in fact, seeing that the "mutated" software caused the machine to stop working completely), the scientists decide to contract with software engineers and programmers to specifically rewrite the code to see if it could be intentionally changed to turn the machine into and operate as a drone (the equivalent of conducting controlled laboratory experiments). After the programmers failed to achieve the task, the scientists would conclude that, given the original structure of the hardware and software, there was no possible way for the machine to be enhanced and reconfigured from the inside out by its own software, and they would write the theory off as a failure.

We can download apps on our smartphones and tablets that allow us to conduct thousands of different complex operations and functions—but we cannot download software into our smartphones that will change them into airplanes or spaceships. Neither the smartphones (hardware) nor the apps (software) are structured to allow for that type of change. We can see in nature that different types of animals come in amazing natural varieties (witness all the types of dogs, birds, and fish) but we have also shown through controlled laboratory experiments that none of the existing biological plants or animals can change into a different type of plant or animal. Neither the biological entities (hardware) nor any of their DNA (software) are structured to allow for that type of change.

The dirty little secret that, given its original structure, it is chemically and biologically impossible for one type of life to "evolve" into a different form of biological life has a number of unsightly appendages hanging off of it as well. As has been documented over and over, genetic mutations in nature do not prove beneficial to the creatures in which they occur. If the genetic code of any given animal was compiled simply by random chance, then we would have every reason to think that changes caused by mutations in that code would, on average, be beneficial fifty percent of the time. If genes, however, were intelligently designed, and the code for each type of life specially set, then we would expect mutations to be beneficial much less frequently—or not at all. Related to this, it is interesting to note that at the beginning of the human race God did not prohibit us from having sexual relations and mating with close relatives. After some time, though, God added commands that humans were not to mate with immediate and some extended family members (Lev. 18:6–13). We now understand that at least part of the reason God put these commands in place was that because over the centuries, genetic mutations had been building up in mankind's genes. If close family members with recessive genetic mutations have offspring, it can cause tremendous harm to their children. This is not only the case with humans but with all animals. English Bulldogs have been so interbred that the breed suffers from the effects of genetic mutations having been passed along from both (too-closely related) parents into the puppies. The cheetah population on the African continent is in danger because of this same reason.

The point is simply this: Genetic mutations are so harmful that the Bible and the legal statutes of the United States prohibit the inbreeding of close human relatives. The biogenetic research of the harmful effects of members of the same species with the same genetic mutations inbreeding are so conclusive that scientists warn those who breed animals against it. So when a scientist claims that it is the inbreeding of certain types of animals with genetic mutations which allow new, more complex creatures to evolve, do they even believe themselves? I do not think they do. How could they? They warn us that in the real world, the inbreeding of parents with similar genetic mutations will have irreversible negative effects on their offspring, but then theoretically state that this exact same process is responsible for all the biological diversity on the planet. Until we hear these scientists recommending inbreeding, we will know that inside they must understand that both parents passing along a similar genetic mutation to their offspring is never a way to increase biological complexity.

The aforementioned atheist-turned-believer in God, Anthony Flew, said in his book entitled *There Is a God*, "natural selection does not positively produce anything. It only eliminates or tends to eliminate whatever is not competitive."[15] In other words, there is no mechanism for producing biological complexity. Natural selection seems to explain only how complex yet non-competitive biological attributes tend to dissipate in biological populations over time—and all scientists and Christians agree with this fact. But how did the biological complexities get there to begin with? And speaking of biological complexity. . . .

As we discussed in chapter 2, the Second Law of Thermodynamics has some nasty implications for the theory of evolution. The understanding that things in our universe are going from a state of increased order to a state of less orderliness presents an obvious challenge to a theory that proposes that biological life has gotten more orderly and more complex over time. The Second Law, in essence, says that things are wearing out, becoming less complex and less structured over time. Even if we don't think about the implications of this for our planet, we all understand this from the surroundings of our daily lives.

Suppose you purchase a new car. Each day, week, month, and year the car wears out a little, so after five years the tires would be fairly well worn. The theory of evolution can be compared to the belief that one of

---

[15] Anthony Flew, *There Is a God* (New York: Harper Collins, 2007), 78.

the tires somehow develops new and better tread as time goes on, while the other three tires and the rest of the car continue to decline (i.e., everything in the universe is wearing out and becoming less ordered—except for biological life on one small planet in a single galaxy). Evolution states that when life first hit earth it was simple, and over time it has grown into increasingly complex and better engineered forms. In other words, the older your car gets and the more you drive it, the newer and better one of the tires becomes. If you walked into your garage and noticed a new tire on one wheel with more sophisticated engineering and tread than what was on the car originally, common sense would tell you that the new tire had to have been intentionally placed there by someone or something else. For those who don't have common sense, we can appeal to the Second Law of Thermodynamics to assure them that the new, better designed tire did not just gradually improve itself over the decade. If—and as we have discussed, that is an impossible if—species change over time into other things as evolution wants to predict, those creatures would be becoming less complex, not more. It is very amusing to listen to certain scientists explain themselves into knots trying to argue their way out of the limitations that the Second Law places on the theory of evolution. Amusing but not convincing.

As stated above, some in science chose to hook their wagon to evolution too soon. They all truly believed at one point that the theory would be validated by biochemistry in the laboratory, and by archeology in the field. Those experiments and discoveries, however, are not validating the theory. Instead they are coming back to bite them. Why did/do they cling to evolution so dearly? There are two interrelated reasons:

- As Amir Aczel puts it in his book *Why Science Does Not Disprove God*, "the New Atheists, who claim to speak for science, are more like religious evangelists bent on converting us to their narrow point of view that God does not exist."[16] The scientists who have

---

[16] Amir Aczel, *Why Science Does Not Disprove God* (New York: William Morrow/Harper Collins, 2014).

made evolution the center of their existence rarely do it in the name of science. Some have supported the theory, and continue to, based on racist motivations (the contention being that those of white, European ancestry are further evolved than people of color—after all, the subtitle of Darwin's book on evolution was *The Preservation of Favoured Races in the Struggle for Life*). But most who have chosen to sacrifice a career at the altar of evolution do so because they do not want there to be a god. Evolution, though not very effective even if true, seemed a possible scientific hope of disproving at least the need for a god in one small area of the vast universe.

- The second reason—or more accurately, Part B of the first reason—is that there were/are not many other areas where even the need for a godlike entity could be ruled out by science. So the scientists to whom this is important hold onto evolution, even in the face of failed experiments and unsupportive archeological finds. With no place else to turn, they simply dig in their heels.

As this book is not designed to be a referendum on the subject, I'll stop here on the topic of evolution. For those interested in reading more, a short list of good books on the subject includes:

> *Evolution: A Theory in Crisis*, by Michael Denton. Originally written in 1985, the main questions with which he challenges evolution have still not been answered by the scientific community.
> *The Edge of Evolution: The Search for the Limits of Darwinism*, by Michael J. Behe
> *Darwin's Black Box*, by Michael J. Behe
> *Darwin on Trial*, by Phillip E. Johnson

Conclusion

As mentioned here and in hundreds of other sources, centuries ago scientists saw their work as a highly Christian activity, because they were literally uncovering the glory of God. They found order and consistency in the universe, definable in terms of the language of mathematics. And this is just what the Bible would have suggested about God's creation, because it says, "For God is not a God of disorder" (1 Cor. 14:33) and "for the Lord is a God of knowledge" (1 Sam. 2:3). As beings created in the image of God to rule over His creation, we were destined to uncover and document the glory of His creation.

Modern science has continued the exploration and documentation of God's creation, and we continue to be amazed by its vastness and beauty. But a detour has been added in just the last few generations. Now some scientists, instead of documenting what exists (and grappling with why), set out to intentionally disprove the notion of God. This is driven by their desire as intellectuals to hold prominent positions and to be revered by other people. Of course, science should not work under the hypothesis that there is or is not a God. Science should simply experiment and document. Wrong conclusions can be made, and money and time wasted, when science is conducted to disprove something which cannot be disproved.

For example, what if scientists, based on the example given earlier in this book about God not wanting the Israelite soldiers to use the bathroom in camp, decided they would not study even the possibility of disease being transmitted by bodily waste, because it would only serve to confirm the Bible? Our knowledge of sanitation would be centuries behind where it is. Fortunately, I don't think scientists knew that was in the Bible, so they unknowingly (and unwillingly) validated the Bible in the process of making breakthroughs in the health sciences.

But though these scientists intentionally set out to achieve a certain level of understanding and by that to disprove the existence of God, they have ended up achieving an even greater level of understanding than imagined, while continually enhancing the likelihood that some "god" type force must exist as the cause of all that we know and see.

When we don't get what we want in life, a basic instinct is to attack someone else. And this is exactly what some modern scientists, frustrated beyond what they could have possibly imagined five decades ago, are resorting to. If someone were to say "I believe the world is flat and sitting on a pedestal," Christians would respond that we always understood, based on verses such as those in Job 26:7–10 and Isaiah 40:21–23, that the earth is suspended in the cosmos ("hangs on nothing") and is shaped more like a 3D circle or a sphere ("inscribing a circle over the face of the waters" and God being "above the circle of the earth"). And scientists would "prove" to this person, using the motion of the planets, our vision over the horizon, pictures from space, and many other things, that the world is not flat and resting on a pedestal.

And if someone says, "Tell me how the world was created, and how life came to be and show me how there came to be so many different life forms," the Christian would say, based on Genesis 1, that an eternal God—who has characteristics and dimensions that cannot be explained by simple science—created all matter and energy and intentionally brought life into existence with one "kind" of living thing being separated from other "kinds" of living things. And the scientists would have to admit that they have no theories (much less proof) of how matter, energy, and life were created. They would have to admit that any explanation would necessarily be a non-scientific, supernatural explanation (which, by definition, is outside the realm of science). And though the scientists would claim to have a theory of how life became so diverse, they would also readily admit that they have not been able to demonstrate or recreate such biological diversity in the laboratory based on this theory.

One can't eliminate the possibility of God and rely only on the discoveries of empirical science to explain the natural world (even if evolution were true) because there are still, at least, four "miracles" required—four phenomena which must have occurred outside the scientific laws that govern our universe:

1. The very existence of matter and energy;
2. A separate energy source for the Big Bang;

3. The occurrence of cosmological inflation immediately after the Big Bang; and

4. The transformation of inanimate matter into biological life

Science not only says that these things occurred outside the scientific laws of nature, but that something large and complex which exists in a dimension undetectable from our universe must have been the catalyst for our universe. That is why multiverse theories have been proposed—because if one simply refuses to consider the possibility of God, something with all the attributes of God (except moral clarity) must be called upon.

Of course, the Bible agrees that something supernatural—an eternal force with great energy and creativity—is responsible for the universe. This same eternal force brought some of the dead matter which had been created to life, using supernatural methods which are beyond those currently governing our universe. The Bible also agrees that this Creator cannot be detected from our universe.

Boiling the issue down to its core, it is easy to see why Christians should be so comfortable with science. The eternal, supernatural force which science says is necessary to explain where everything came from and how some of it came to life is the God of the Bible. The harder scientists have worked to show that there is no need for God to explain things in the universe, the more they have fulfilled the messages of Matthew 2 and Romans 1 by showing people through the study of the universe that there is a need for an eternal, miraculous God.

CHAPTER 7

The View of Medicine

Given the complimentary view of science and the contributions it has made to mankind presented in the previous chapter, it is understandable that those with a biblical worldview would have a very positive view of medicine as well.

There are a couple of places in the New Testament where medical practices are mentioned in a positive light. One is the story of the Good Samaritan in Luke 10. The story itself was told by Jesus as a denunciation of racism (because the players involved were of different races; more on that in chapter 8), but was based on the setup of one person traveling down a road and seeing another person who had been mugged and left badly beaten up on the side of the road. Jesus says that the person poured oil and wine on the injured man's wounds (in other words, used the best medicines available at that time) and wrapped him in bandages (utilizing the best medical equipment available at that time). At the end of the story, Jesus says that we should all go and act the same way as this man did. Jesus did not say that the man was wrong to use medicine, or that the man should have just prayed for God to heal the injured man.

The simple fact is that God performed miracles through people and for people to authenticate His message and His messengers. God never promised miraculous help to believers on every occasion, even for curing health issues. If you have ever been in a pre-op room when an evangelical preacher prays before someone's surgery, you will have noticed that they pray that the surgeons are guided as they perform the operation and that the medicine is effective in healing the person's body; of course, they also pray for the family and their mental state, etc. These pastors know that they can ask God for a miracle, but they have no right to demand one or (only) rely on one. More than asking for a miracle, they pray that God's providence, through the use of people's talents and the medicines which have been concocted over time, is effective in healing the sick person.

This is not the book to discuss the theology of how God works in the world through providence and natural causes as opposed to miracles that defy nature—other than to state that those with a biblical worldview, leaning only on what God has revealed in the Bible, understand that miracles are highly unlikely to occur today. The purpose (and therefore the time) for miracles as described in the Bible has passed. Those who say that you just have to have faith have a disturbing misunderstanding of how the Bible defines that term. In biblical books such as Romans (chapter 4) and Hebrews (chapter 11), faith is defined as believing that God will do the things that He has promised (things such as allowing the righteousness of Christ to be granted to our account if we repent, and that Christ will return for His followers one day) and believing that God will reward those who seek Him, even though they can't see Him and the reward will usually come in the afterlife. God simply did not promise to heal all people who get sick and ask to be made well. If He did, I suppose the apostles and other faithful Christians would have never died!

The Bible is actively opposed to defining faith as our believing that God is going to do whatever we ask of Him. That is simply too self-centered to be biblical. God does not exist to wait on and fulfill our next request. It is more in tune with Scripture to understand that faith is still believing that God is in control of the final outcome of the universe, and will ultimately use all things for good to those who choose to follow Him, even when we are hurting and don't see the positive in the situation (see Habakkuk 2:4 and Romans 8:28). In other words, true faith is not thinking that I can live however risky a lifestyle I choose and ignore all medical help, then pray in faith and always be healed. True faith is not always understanding why things turned out the way they did, even though I lived right and got the best help, but believing in the love and control of God in spite of my misunderstanding. A huge portion of the stories in the Bible are designed to show us how things worked out for God's followers in the past, even though they could not see the results in their own lifetimes.

As an example, think about someone feeding their family. It is unbiblical for a parent to say that they have faith that if they pray to God, He will provide food for their family without them lifting a finger. That is not the definition of biblical faith; that is the definition of total laziness and insanity. God allows us to eat the meat of animals, and has provided seasons, soil, rain, and crops to help feed us. God also made us in His image, and part of that means that we are active, creative beings. God will absolutely allow us to develop better farming techniques and better farming equipment with which to feed ourselves. If someone said, "Please pray that my family is fed this week, because we are very hungry and have been sitting in our living room faithfully waiting for God to fill our stomachs with no luck yet," it would not take a Bible scholar to tell them that the whole concept they have about what God does for people and how He does it is mixed up. Likewise, if someone says that they want to be healed without using any of the latest medical techniques, drugs, or equipment because they are sitting in the living room waiting faithfully for God to heal them, we should again tell them that they have a mixed-up notion of what God does for people and why and how He does it.

In an example from the Old Testament portion of the Bible (Isaiah 38), the terminally ill king Hezekiah was promised by God (after praying about it) that he would survive his illness and be allowed to live another fifteen years. After being told that his prayer had been answered, the best medicine available (a poultice made of figs, in this case) was applied before the king was healed. So the best biblical examples show that, even when God does directly answer a prayer for healing, the healing is normally brought to fruition by the effectiveness and application and the best available manmade medicine.

The simple truth is: We should take advantage of modern medicine and surgical procedures as gifts from God. No one should avoid being treated by doctors any more than they should avoid eating food from a field which was plowed by a manmade device or treated with fertilizer (including good old-fashioned manure). God did not promise to automatically fill your stomach, and God did not promise to automatically heal your sickness. As creation made in His image, we are allowed to think and improve upon our techniques and procedures over time in the areas He has granted to us, including medicine.

At this point, I know that many people are asking, "But what about Aunt Jane, who was cured by a miracle?" I do not want to sound coarse or sarcastic, but I would think that ninety-nine percent of the people who were thought to be cured by a miracle were actually just misdiagnosed by the doctor. Modern medicine is advanced and complex, but each person and each occurrence of a disease is unique, and no doctor is perfect. When the weather forecast is wrong, we do not conclude that it must have been a miracle of God for the weather to have been different than what was predicted. In many cases, it is probably easier to predict the weather five days out than the course someone's disease is going to take over the next six months. However, when a doctor says that there is little chance the tumor will shrink or the patient will only live for three more months and the tumor goes away and the patient lives for years, it is often labeled as a miracle.

I think there are probably three main reasons people tend to feel that God should be, and therefore must be, working miraculously in the realm of healthcare today (not one of which have much biblical standing):

1. We want a sign from God; we want to see His power on display somehow. Jesus bitterly condemned people, though, who let this type of attitude go too far (Matt. 16:1–4). Christians are to trust God based on His record of accuracy and historical prophecy fulfillment. We are to trust in His love for us based on the fact that Christ was willing to die for us (Rom. 5:8). For a biblically accurate description of how a modern Christian can experience God, see Henry & Richard Blackaby and Claude King's book *Experiencing God.*

2. We tend to think that because health issues—especially those which cross between life and death—are so important (to us) that they must be in a separate category when it comes to God and how He is dealing with mankind today. In fact, God is dealing with mankind in those categories which are the most important to *Him*. Those categories involve people's souls, however, and not their physical health. The Bible says that God is active in convicting people of their sin and their need for salvation through Jesus (John 16:7–11; Rev. 3:20), and that He continues to call people to Him (Acts 2:39). From a human viewpoint, nothing seems more important than for a person to be healed who is sick enough to die. But from God's superior viewpoint, He knows that the separate category He must work on is having people give all moral authority to Him (repenting) as a way to accept the grace of Jesus Christ through faith.

3. A misunderstanding of how we are to apply the stories of the miracle healings in the New Testament to our lives today.

Regarding this third reason, allow me to make a few extra points. First, I do believe that many (maybe most) of the events called "signs and wonders" in the Bible were true miracles. In many cases, though, it appears that God used events within the realm of nature to further His causes. Examples might be earthquakes, or the fact that the giant slain by the young boy David, Goliath, likely had the growth disorder acromegaly, causing him to be tall but also limiting his peripheral vision and making the temple area on his head much more sensitive to outside blows. But there are specific cases in the Bible, especially at the start of each new era of miracles (those beginning with the exodus of the Jews from Egypt, those beginning with the age of the prophets under Elijah, and those beginning with Jesus and His apostles), where the Bible states that these signs and wonders were not only miracles but designed and executed in such a way that they could not be denied by nonbelievers, replicated, or explained away. I believe Jesus' miracle healings were just that: miracles. But I can believe that some misread what that means for our faith today.

Before we examine this point further, I feel as though it would first be helpful to go back and look at another episode and see what it has to teach us today. The second book of the Bible, Exodus, tells the story of the Hebrews being delivered from slavery in the land of Egypt. Being helpless to deliver themselves, God intervened on their behalf, securing a method for their freedom. Once outside the realm of Egyptian control, God established a method through which the fledgling Hebrew nation could undertake sacrifices to atone for their sins, if only temporarily. Is our lesson from this Scripture that God is going to deliver us from physical slavery (if we ever find ourselves in that predicament) and provide a way for us to temporarily escape the consequences of our sins? No! The common ground of what was being foreshadowed in these events is our freedom from the slavery of sin, and the permanent payment for the debt of those sins in the ultimate sacrifice to come by Jesus.

To cope with life, we all build certain escape hatches and comfortable routines into our existence. These include not just drugs or alcohol but anger, cussing, breaking off healthy relationships too early or staying in unhealthy relationships too long, etc. Often these attempts to deal with the difficulty of reality become harmful themselves. Too many times they become destructive habits or addictions which enslave us. They literally take us as slaves in this life and have eternal consequences as well. The lesson from the exodus of the Jews during the time of Moses is that God provides for us—in advance and solely out of His mercy—a way out of both the slavery of our sinful habits and the eternal consequences associated with them.

With this as a background, is the lesson of Jesus and His apostles healing sick people meant to teach us that we are to get physical healing directly from Jesus or His modern-day leaders? No! The common ground being foreshadowed here is actually very similar to the previous example. When you come to have biblical faith in Christ—what is referred to in the New Testament as "believing in the name of the Son of God" or "repenting"—you realize these sins which enslave you are, in a sense, an illness. Modern science has now figured out what the Bible taught all along: Your mind can change your brain (again, for more information read *The Brain That Changes Itself* by Norman Doidge and/ or *Switch on Your Brian* by Caroline Leaf). That is, the decisions you make, the deepest desires of your heart, even the thoughts that you dwell on, physically change the wiring in your brain.

This act of repenting, turning toward God, and seeking to understand His method for living your life leaves you concerned that you have become a person so sick with sin that has been wired into your brain that there is no way to be healed again. We come to understand that we can defeat any habit we have developed, but that if we do not cure ourselves of the underlying cause (or "illness") which triggered the habit to begin with, we will simply trade one habit for another. I can stop smoking but I start eating and gain weight; I can stop drinking but I have to withdraw from social settings because they make me too anxious in a sober state of mind. And the list of tradeoffs we deal with in our lives goes on and on. Also, almost everyone reading this book will at one time or another have recognized that they have put a bad habit behind them only to have it reoccur during a time of stress or pain. It turns out that the habit itself is not your disease; it is a symptom of the disease. Alcoholism, addiction to sex, or frequent episodes of uncontrolled anger are the result of the real disease, which is a life unattached from the will of God. All humans have the "disease," and display at least mild symptoms of it.

In the friendship and support that I have tried to lend to people struggling with addictions or other life-altering habits, I have found that only a minority of individuals defeat the habit without replacing it with another habit (though usually a much less destructive habit, at least) and/or without relapsing at some point in their life. This has been true of people I have dealt with inside and outside the church. This has been true of individuals who have gone through a government-mandated twelve-step program such as Narcotics Anonymous, a church-based twelve-step program such as Saddleback Church's Celebrate Recovery or those who have used a non-twelve-step approach such as those developed by the intriguing academic research of psychologists such as Stanton Peele. The reason so many folks fail or struggle for so long before they succeed is that they are working on a symptom and not the under-lying disease. I can feel a fever, and so I may identify that as my medical problem. Treating it with aspirin or acetaminophen, however, will only cause temporary relief if the underlying illness is a bacterial infection somewhere in my body. I need antibiotics to cure the infection, and aspirin to deal with the symptoms.

Whenever God broke into history to enhance how He managed His relationship with man, He always allowed miracles to be performed to vali-date that it was Him relaying a new message, and to give credibility to those who were speaking the message for Him. The reason that Jesus and His apostles were able to perform miracles was to announce a message from God—that Jesus was the Christ who would save mankind from their sins and break the shackles of the sin disease that holds them in slavery. The reason that some of those miracles included people rising from the dead (including Jesus Himself) was to announce in advance that through repen-tance and faith in Jesus, the consequence of our disease (suffering spiritual death after our physical death) was conquered. The fact that so many of those miracles were healings of sickness were to help us understand, that through faith in His love and ability, we can have a true healing of the dis-ease that afflicts our hearts and minds while we are still living on the earth.

Did Jesus raising Lazarus from the dead relay the message to all Christian believers that we will never die physically because we will always be miraculously revived? No! The primary purpose of that mira-cle was to validate Jesus as the Son of God. The secondary purpose was to foreshadow that Jesus was going to conquer spiritual death for us, not physical death. Were the healings of sick people a message (or even a guarantee) that Christians will be miraculously healed by God? No! The primary purpose of those miracles was to validate Jesus as the Son of God. The secondary purpose was to foreshadow that an even more important healing, a spiritual healing, was coming to mankind through faith in Jesus Christ. As the apostle Paul wrote:

> But thanks be to God, that you who were once slaves of
> sin have become obedient from the heart to the standard of

teaching to which you were committed, and, having been set free from sin, have become slaves of righteousness. I am speaking in human terms, because of your natural limitations. For just as you once presented your members as slaves to impurity and to lawlessness leading to more lawlessness, so now present your members as slaves to righteousness leading to sanctification. For when you were slaves of sin, you were free in regard to righteousness. But what fruit were you getting at that time from the things of which you are now ashamed? For the end of those things is death. But now that you have been set free from sin and have become slaves of God, the fruit you get leads to sanctification and its end, eternal life. For the wages of sin is death, but the free gift of God is eternal life in Christ Jesus our Lord (Rom. 6:17–23).

Jesus' healings are to show us that through faith in Christ we can be healed. The foreshadowing was literal, physical healing (just as its predecessor was literal, physical slavery), but our lesson is that we are not doomed to a life trapped by previous decisions and only able to deal with the symptoms of our disease. If we repent, turn toward God's ways, and seek His counsel for living through faith, Jesus will help to heal us of the underlying sickness from which all humans suffer.

Of course, there is a very small subpopulation of religious folks who have a mistaken and distorted view of medicine altogether. Their view and the results of it are exceptionally sad. And their view of the teachings of the Bible—believing that God has promised to miraculously heal, and that this is the only way believers are allowed to seek healing—is, as the previous pages have documented, not biblical at all.

Those with a biblical worldview use modern medicine and modern medical techniques (and thank God for their existence). We encourage medical as well as scientific research. We do not require the medicine we take to have been developed to be Christians, nor the doctors we employ. The Bible does not tell us that we should remove ourselves from the world and isolate in Bible-believing communities, buying and selling only from others of similar faith. In fact, it teaches us just the opposite.

Of course, there is the outstanding matter of bioethics—stem cell research, end-of-life issues, etc. These will be dealt with in the next chapter.

CHAPTER 8

The View of Social and Legal Issues

There are too many detailed subjects under this heading to provide anything approaching a comprehensive review. Therefore, I will cover ten broad topics as a way to demonstrate the general thinking on some common legal and social issues by those with a biblical worldview.

Political Correctness

Whether you ask Christians or non-Christians, most would agree that as a general rule, Evangelicals are not viewed as being particularly politically correct. Political correctness at its core has turned out to be a way for people to pick on their opponents and try to make them look bad, rather than a way to promote what is helpful and beneficial. In most areas covered by the haze of political correctness today, opinions vary and details change quickly. Keeping up with what is politically correct becomes a nightmare. In so many cases where charges of insensitivity due to political incorrectness are made, accusers are just looking for an excuse to pounce on someone they have already identified as an enemy.

There are a few issues in this category, however, which are broad-based and longstanding examples of one group of people mistreating or mislabeling another, and where we are in agreement with the mainstream politically correct movement.

One major issue involves the Confederate flag, and some of the state flags in the Southeast which are based on the "stars and bars" of the Confederate flag. Simply stated, we do not approve of the things those flags stand for. Some of these state flags were not around during the Civil War, but were created much later as a protest of sorts. We are not asking that people give up a meaningful portion of their history. But we do support replacing Southern state flags with new designs and ask that people consider removing or limiting the use of the Confederate flag. It has become a divisive symbol, and a large number of people see it as downright hateful. Of course, we understand that different individuals will have different opinions, but our biblical worldview dictates that we be sensitive to the feelings of others where that is possible (Rom. 12:18).

A counter-example would be voter ID laws. Many local and national commentators have spoken out against these laws, suggesting that they are discriminatory, divisive, and a hateful reminder of past racial discrimination. But the overwhelming majority of those with a biblical worldview that I have spoken to are either neutral or in support of voter ID laws. Early results suggest that minority voting has not been hampered in the locations where voter ID laws have been implemented, and it is just so important that we can trust our elections in America.

For another example of political correctness and race, consider Stone Mountain Park. It sits just outside of Atlanta, Georgia. Into the side of the mountain are carved two Confederate generals and the president of the old Confederacy. The streets inside the park have names such as Confederate Avenue. Honestly, it surprises me that people inside and outside of Georgia do not appear to see this as being more politically incorrect. Robert E. Lee, one of the three men carved into Stone Mountain, is considered by some to be the greatest traitor in the history of our country. He probably ranks with individuals such as Benedict Arnold, Julius and Ethel Rosenberg, and Aaron Burr. Robert E. Lee was a graduate of the United States Military Academy at West Point and served for decades in the US Army before defecting to the Confederacy. America is the greatest country in the history of the world, and we should not celebrate those who have taken up arms against it or tried to destroy its greatness.

There is another area where evangelicals should have sympathy with the politically correct crowd. This is in their opposition to sports teams which use Native American names and mascots. Their reasoning is the same as before. If the names or the silly mascots imply negative things about a group of people or are viewed by those individuals as hateful or shameful, then why not just give them up and change the team name to something which does not inflict these feelings on others? Again, those Christians opposed to the Atlanta Braves or Washington Redskins are not calling for legal mandates to force changes. It is just their opinion that such names are not preferred.

Environmental Issues

During my fifty years on the earth, I have heard of one environmental "scare" after another—none of which have come to fruition. I will not spend much time here writing about the successive waves of issues, and why they did not cause the harm predicted by the fearmongers who so publicly broadcasted them. For those interested in greater detail on these issues, I highly recommend that you read the books *The Skeptical Environmentalist* by Bjorn Lumborg and *The Rational Optimist* by Matt Ridley. I believe these books should be required reading in all high schools and colleges. Patrick Allitt's fair and objective book *A Climate of Crisis* is definitely worth reading as well.

When I was a young child, there was a repeated threat that the world was going to run out of food, from a combination of too many people and declining food production. Today we have enough food to feed everyone in the world; we just cannot get governments out of the way to get it distributed. As I watched the Saturday morning nature programs while I was in middle school, there was always a list of endangered animals discussed, and the list grew and grew in size. The reason that these animals were going to disappear was always because humans were destroying their habitat. As I look around the globe now, I realize that all of those animals that humans would destroy are still here. All of them! The last time I spoke to a practicing biologist, he told me that new species become extinct every year but that humans had directly eliminated very few animals from earth over time, and that it had probably been one hundred years since humans eliminated their last species from earth—carrier pigeons in the early 1900s (due to overhunting).

The theme of running out of stuff has been a constant threat from the environmental corner. I have been told we are running out of safe drinking water, running out of clean air, and running out of oil. Again, we have run out of none of these things over time. The air now is cleaner than it has been over the last couple of centuries, and there are more known oil reserves in the ground today than at any other time in history. Additionally, there has been explosive growth in the known reserves of natural gas in just the last few years.

When I was in high school, we were told that global cooling was going to grip the European continent, and that the results were going to be awful (check the old news stories; it's true). For a number of years after that, we were told that global warming was the problem. But global warming's credibility started to suffer and the "false prophets" now use the phrase "climate change" instead. Depending on your source of data, for something like fifteen out of the last eighteen years, average global temperatures have not gone up. And then there are the "Climategate" emails which show that global warming's supporters are nervous enough about the theory that they are trying to control the communications about it. My guess is that in another ten to fifteen years we won't be hearing about global warming or climate change anymore, and there will be a new threat on the horizon.

The Bible tells us that we are stewards of God's earth. Humans are literally to be the onsite managers of what ultimately belongs to God, and we are to take care of what He has entrusted to us, using it for our benefit without wasting it or needlessly destroying it. Some environmentalists have questioned whether there is some biblical reason that evangelical Christians are not more aligned with them. My lack of urgent concern about these issues, though, is not directly biblical but is simply based on the historical data. Time and again I have heard of the potential problems, and time and again they turn out to be overblown. The groups which would be broadly labeled as environmentalists or conservationists have lost a tremendous amount of credibility with those who are keeping track of their predictions. (Remember that both Moses and Jesus warned us in the Bible about "false prophets" whose predictions never quite seem to come true.) Two interesting reads on this subject are Troy Lacey's online article "Is Stewardship the Same as Going Green?" and Paul Sabin's book *The Bet*.

We all want to live in a world that is as clean and safe as possible, and everyone can understand the value of conservation. But an obvious question to ask is: Why do some people continue to overstate the environmental threats we face in our future, especially when their track record is so poor? For this, I do have a direct biblical answer.

Point 18 in chapter 3 states that God has put "eternity in the hearts of man." Not only were we built to understand a God is out there, but we are wired to want to make an impact on something bigger than ourselves. The Bible tells us that somewhere inside us, each of us wants to leave a lasting impact. God's way is that we do this through impacting His kingdom. This earth will ultimately pass away, and only things related to the salvation of people's souls and the heavenly kingdom will last for eternity. But most of us do not naturally think in these terms; we seek to make our lasting impact through our children, through successes that will be written about in the history books, or by getting our name on a building or a long-lasting foundation. In having conversations with folks who were self-labeled environmentalists, I have noticed that many of them speak in the grand terms of someone who wants to be involved in something bigger than themselves. They want their lives to matter and their influence to outlive them. A few of them simply have a need to feel morally superior to others and use environmental causes as a way to establish (at least in their own mind) that they are truly better people. But most, I think, really want to do good things that make a long-term difference.

I believe it is this pressure they put on themselves to improve the world they live in that causes so many of them to place unrealistic importance on environmental and conservation issues and which causes them to be unwilling to admit when their scary forecasts are wrong. Almost unknown to them, they allow the issues they champion to take on a larger-than-reality role in their own minds, and find it hard to let go of an issue even when evidence no longer supports it.

Christians understand that God has made us stewards of His earth. We are to multiply and fill the earth, subdue it and manage it for God. I want to be a good steward in that regard, just as I want to use my life in every other way that God has commanded me. But simply put, we come down differently in our opinion of environmental/conservation issues than many others do. We have not assigned an outrageous importance to those issues and therefore do not take extreme opinions, call for extreme measures, or defend any opinions or measures beyond reason. If too many trees are being cut down in one area, or a certain species is being overfished, we will join the call to take prudent action. But we do not suggest that drastic action be taken to eliminate automobiles because of a suggested lack of oil, or that we close down half the businesses in the country and leave our houses unheated in winter to help keep global warming at bay. While we are all for using more and more natural gas for generating electricity and powering vehicles as times progress and technologies allow, as it stands today, we are okay with using coal for electricity where needed and gasoline for cars.

Although recycling is a popular, feel-good initiative in today's world, driven by environmental concerns, many studies have shown that the energy and materials consumed are equal to or even greater than the energy and materials saved in recycling programs in most areas. Many Christians recycle, but we understand that we are not really saving the world through doing it. Christians do agree, though, with general conservation guidelines. We do not think that we have to build the biggest houses, drive the largest gas-guzzling cars, or take extremely long vacations in the most far-away locations. Each person should conserve energy where they can, but it is okay to fire up some natural gas to make the energy we need.

As you read the Scriptures of the New Testament, it becomes obvious that Jesus had ongoing issues with the religious leaders of His day. It also becomes obvious that the major reason for His disagreements with them was their hypocrisy, generated by their need to feel self-righteous. Today we see that same issue with too many environmentalists and conservationists. Conservative writers love to make fun of Al Gore for his multiple homes and heated pools, or Angelina Jolie for the vacations she takes and the private transportation she utilizes, etc. But all hypocrisy in the environmental and conservation arenas are not laughing matters. Read the book *Eco-Imperialism: Green Power Black Death* by Paul Driessen for an overview of such issues.

It is shocking how many commentators have suggested or outright stated that the billions of people in developing countries should be subject to strict regulations about what fuels they can power their growing economies with, how they can fertilize their food, and on and on. If rich Americans want to lobby within this country for stricter controls on power plants, outlawing SUVs, or even setting legal limits on the temperature at which we each can set our thermostats—and they are willing to set the pace and obey these laws—then they are free to do so within the political framework of the United States (though I do not think the public or the courts would have much sympathy for their maneuvers). But to call on the poor in Haiti and various African countries, or the very poor in India or China, to face restrictions in their economic growth now that we have achieved *our* growth is hypocrisy at its absolute worst. Dozens of officials in poor countries have been complaining for decades that what we call environmentalism in America is a rich person's (hypocritical) concern. When America was struggling to gain political and economic freedom, and then working through the process of becoming a wealthy, developed country, we put no such restrictions on ourselves. Neither should we call for restrictions on those nations which are currently developing.

To give some idea of where the average evangelical Christian stands on such issues, consider the use of the infamous chemical DDT in controlling the spread of malaria through the eradication of the mosquitoes which carry it. America and other developed nations utilized DDT to help eliminate the existence of malaria and the hideous effects of the disease. Though there are safer, off-shoot versions of the chemical today, the environmental movement had its use banned in America, and pressures other countries to limit or ban its use as well. I truly believe that if malarial mosquitoes became a problem in the US and a million children of rich conservationists suffered and died from the disease every year, Americans would magically come up with a reason to bring the use of DDT or some related chemical back into use for a while. When those millions of kids suffering tragically from fevers and dying before the prime of their life are poor African kids, however, too many folks want to stand on their moral high ground. Every person I have spoken to over the last year (literally every single one of them) who thinks that I am crazy for saying it is okay to use DDT in Africa all say that the reason they oppose it is because it would end up killing too many birds (as the accumulation of DDT in the bodies of many species of birds causes a thinning of their egg shells). I have mentioned to every single one of them that an article in the *LA Times* quotes the Fish and Wildlife Service as estimating that wind turbines in America (used to generate electricity) kill 440,000 birds a year (an article in *The Wall Street Journal* suggested it was closer to 570,000 birds per year, including more than 80,000 protected birds of prey). I ask them if they are okay with all these bird deaths, especially given that wind generates only one-half of one percent of all the country's electricity. They all said "yes." To see how far they would go, I asked them would they be comfortable if all the electricity in the US was generated by wind power, implying that 88,000,000 birds would be killed each year in the blades of the turbines. They all said yes again! In fact, they said they would prefer that all electricity were made by either water or wind. If the loss of 88 million birds—every year!—is not a problem, then how can the possible loss of a few hundred thousand birds in Africa be such a big deal when five-year-olds are dying of a preventable disease? I guess the good moral feeling from replacing coal with wind power is greater than that of saving birds, which in turn is greater than saving poor African kids from an untimely and unnecessary death.

The point is that Christians are all for being sensible about conservation issues, but we have to strongly consider the impact that any environmental moves will have on human lives, now and in the future. We are afraid to stand in judgment before Jesus if we have been hypocritical in life by asking others to undergo conditions that we have not or would not be willing to submit to ourselves.

Drugs

From the conversation in chapter 4 about alcohol prohibition and drugs, you can probably guess where I am going with this one. Though fathers abandoning their families have caused the most devastation I have seen in my lifetime, I can truthfully say that drug and alcohol abuse is not far behind. Far too many of the young men in my church and community, whom I have tried to counsel and mentor, have had their lives nearly destroyed by parents who have substance addiction and abuse problems. These young men share no fault in this tragedy; they are simply caught in a hideous spiral which is brutal in its consequences. I absolutely hate what the misuse of drugs and alcohol have done to our society. I feel bad for the abusers who get caught in the wicked cycle of drugs, and bad for those around them who suffer and enable them.

However, there are a number of things which make me sad, and from which the young men I try to work with have suffered. As stated above, everything harmful cannot be outlawed, and the positive effects from making an action illegal must be weighed against the difficulty of enforcing the law and any direct and indirect negative costs or consequences of the law. As with alcohol, many evangelical Christians today seriously debate whether America's drug policy is really viable in its current form. Of course, changing the laws to say that no substance is illegal to anyone of any age wouldn't work either—likely making things far, far worse than they are now.

We absolutely are not claiming that the answers are easy; we are just suggesting that every alternative be examined and very carefully weighed. The death toll from the illegal drug trade is staggering. The power attained by the growers and distributers of illegal drugs is frightening. When alcohol was made illegal in the US in the 1920s, the country saw a sharp spike in extremely violent organized crime activity. Innocent people were hurt, dangerous people were gaining in wealth and power, and yet alcohol continued to be consumed. Something must change with America's drug laws. So much time and money are spent, so many prisons built, so many innocent lives lost, and so many ruthless people have money, power, and influence under the current drugs laws and yet drugs continue to be used by millions.

Of course, if you commit other crimes while high on drugs, Christians are happy to see stiff penalties imposed. Whether it is driving while under the influence of drugs, stealing, or fighting related to drugs, all those things should be punished.

As stated over and over again in this book, the Bible warns us about being self-righteous. When those with a biblical worldview think about drug laws, we have to be careful that we are not calling for policies to be enacted because it makes us feel morally good (or even morally superior) to stand against such an evil thing. If society benefits the most from the current drug laws, then leave them as they are. But if in some ways the costs outweigh the benefits, let's put the pros and cons on the scale and determine a new, better approach. As an opening volley: Should marijuana—prescribed by a doctor for medical purposes—be legal or not? I would say that it should, for many of the reasons stated above.

Justice / Prison Sentences / Capital Punishment

By "justice," the Bible does not mean that we believe in forgiving everyone's crimes and letting them go free. The Bible explicitly states that to leave a crime unpunished is as bad as punishing an innocent person (for example, see Proverbs 17:15; 18:5; 19:19; and 24:23–25). Throughout the Bible, we are taught that, because of weaknesses in human nature, incentives matter. Allowing a person, or someone else who is observing that person, to come to think that they can commit crimes without any consequences is wrong. Justice in the biblical sense simply means that people understand what the rules are and are treated the same way under those rules, no matter who they are.

This has two different components. The first is that people understand the rules and need to be knowingly committing a crime. Many libertarians in the country are (rightfully) upset that the federal legal code has grown so complex and obscure that people are being arrested nearly every day for having breeched the goofiest laws, of which they had no intention to violate. If I am skipping rocks with my kids at the lake, I do not want us all to be arrested for violating some archeological law about not tampering with items which might fall under the category of protected arrowheads.

The second biblical component was intentionally written into America's founding documents. We believe that people should be treated the same, no matter what their status. And we believe that you should want people treated the same, no matter what their relation is to you. That is true biblical justice. If you had mistakenly told the Kennedy family that when those two people drove off a bridge near Chappaquiddick Island and one of them swam to safety but did not immediately report the accident—and it was their relative Ted Kennedy who was the person left behind found dead, drowned in the car—do you think how they desired to see the survivor treated would have been different than when they found out Ted was actually the one alive and that Mary Jo Kopechne was the one who was found dead?

To make it closer to home, what if someone told you that a person had committed a violent crime against your child, husband, or mother and had caused them serious injury? How would you want them prosecuted? How should they pay for their crime? After deciding what you thought was appropriate process and punishment, would you change your mind if you found out that the one who committed the violent crime was your family member, and that it was someone else who was badly hurt? Almost everyone would set two different criteria in place. If your child is going to walk with a limp the rest of their life, mercy will likely be far from your mind. But if your child has harmed someone else (giving them the same lifelong limp), wouldn't you immediately start making excuses for why the punishment should be less severe? It is the desire and ability to apply laws and consequences equally that the Bible defines as justice, and it is a very difficult concept for us to uphold in our personal lives or in our court system. However, we should certainly try.

As a general rule, those with a biblical worldview probably desire tougher sentencing than the average person. We cannot escape the fact that so many people who commit crimes early continue to commit them over time, and usually commit crimes of increasing severity as the years pass. Juveniles who commit violent person-to-person acts should be charged as adults. We certainly agree that young people who "slip up" should be given a second chance. But those who violently cause physical harm to others, even at very young ages, should be incarcerated for a long time. We are not opposed to the types of laws which say that after a certain number of violent convictions, a criminal cannot be re-released into society.

Though we are opposed to inmates having access to things such as pornography, we fully support all educational initiatives. We like to see addiction recovery, anger management, and religious seminars offered in prisons as well. We are adamant that prisoners must be protected from each other and from the overuse of force by guards. Inmates who create dangerous conditions for other inmates must be harshly dealt with and segregated from the population. They are in prison for a reason and should serve out their time, both as a punishment for the crime committed and to keep them off the streets for a time, in the hope that they can be educated/rehabilitated. But their punishment should be under the steady hand of the government and not at the discretion of other inmates. I have known of a couple of former prisoners who had more power and control, and used it to torment more people inside the jail than they did outside the jail. That is a horrible outcome and we must guard against it.

According to both the Bible and the US Constitution, capital punishment is allowed. As individuals, we are not allowed to take someone's life proactively. But if we are acting in self-defense, or if a soldier or law enforcement officer is acting on behalf of the government, it is allowed, according to scripture and US law. Christians today are split on this issue, however, because of the concern over its just application. Some evangelicals are opposed to capital punishment because they are concerned that a disproportionately high number of blacks are given the death penalty, relative to whites for the exact same crime. Others have recently grown opposed to capital punishment because they are concerned by the number of murder and rape convictions that are being overturned by DNA evidence (for examples, research the *Innocence Project*). There are quite a few Christians, though, who support the application of the death penalty as long as it is applied under the appropriate structure. In either case, the Bible itself supports the idea of life in prison without parole, as well as the death penalty.

Stem Cell Research

The quick and easy statement about stem cell research is that we support it. There are exciting, perhaps revolutionary discoveries to be made and medical cures to be developed through stem cell research. The natural stem cells in our bodies play a unique and critical role in maintaining our health. If the design and function of stem cells can be harnessed by science and leveraged by medicine, millions of people worldwide will benefit.

Our statement on embryonic stem cell research is just as quick and easy: We do *not* support it! There are essentially two types of stem cells used in research: those collected from live adult tissue (for which our understanding of the types and usage grows every day), and those collected from embryo tissue after the embryo has been killed. The recent breakthroughs and possible future discoveries with adult stem cell research are very exciting. But to kill a human to use its body parts in laboratory research is simply wrong. How could it not be!

I do not have a problem with a living person donating a kidney or a portion of their liver to another person who is physically sick, nor do I object to organ donor programs which allow those who have passed away in a hospital to have their organs (corneas, livers, hearts, etc.) donated to another person. I would have a tremendous problem, however, if we allowed a forceful person to harvest organs for themselves from weaker persons who could not stop the action from happening. Just because you can catch me, kill me, pay a doctor to take my organs (or stem cells) out, and then use them for your benefit, it does not mean that it should be allowed. Christians have an obligation to stand up for those who cannot defend themselves. Embryos which are created to be killed in the name of medical science cannot speak on their own, but I can loudly and boldly say that it is sad that our society would treat them in this way.

Genetically Modified Food

There is no biblical problem with genetically modified foods (usually referred to as GMO). In fact, to date, the only thing accomplished by those who protest and call for boycotts on these foods, is that kids in developing countries continue to go to bed hungry. For thousands and thousands of years, in places as diverse as France, Mexico, Ukraine, and Peru, people have been breeding crops (accidently and intentionally) to produce new genetic varieties of the foods that we all eat. To use scientific processes to make the genetic modifications that allow certain crops to become more nutritional, or to grow in harsher climates, follows the biblical principles that we should be creative, subdue the earth and have dominion over it, managing it for the benefit of other humans to the glory of God.

GMOs have not proven dangerous to people or planet Earth. Somehow, though, opposing GMOs became a socially acceptable way to prove one's environmental credentials. This movement has been fueled in part by the likes of celebrities such as Bill Nye (the self-proclaimed "Science Guy"), who maintained a public suspicion about GMOs for years, writing about it in books and discussing it in interviews. Though his opposition seems to have lessened over the last few years, it is unclear what caused him to take such a stance to begin with. But whether it was irrational beliefs, personal opinion, or weakening under public pressure, those with a biblical worldview would encourage him to stand on the side of the facts. Based on the combination of biblical precepts and current scientific testing, those with a biblical worldview continue to support GMOs and look forward to the continued and growing benefit they will bring to mankind.

End-of-Life Issues

Discussions among evangelical Christians about assisted suicide for those struggling with pain and debilitation near the end of their life are very interesting. To be quite frank, we feel stuck on the issue. Obviously we do not like to watch others suffer, and fear the possibility that it will happen to us. Of course, we have no issue with aggressive pain management, using the latest medical drugs and techniques. Ultimately, though, we all seem to come back to the conclusion that we are playing God if we decide for ourselves or a close loved one to intentionally end a life, even one where the person is suffering horribly. Having come to that conclusion among a group of believers, if you started up the same conversation that next day, the discussion would be long and lively again as they pored over the same agonizing details. Ultimately, though, they are going to come to the same conclusion: Manage the pain, and let God decide about life and death in those instances.

In instances where a child is born with defects or a person has an accident and becomes immobile, we also believe that life must be preserved and cherished. In 2005, a case involving a woman named Terri Schiavo made national headlines as her life was ended when her feeding tube was removed and she passed away from starvation and dehydration. Evangelical Christians were quite vocal in our opposition to her death. We are not, however, opposed to "pulling the plug" on someone who is only being kept alive by the impulses of a machine. These issues get tricky for everybody, so allow me an illustration.

Consider the following scenario: After a crash landing on an island involving you and one other person, you walk away without a scratch and the other person is badly injured. If that person has broken both arms and both legs, an evangelical would say that we should go around the island collecting the necessary food and water for both of us, and then feeding the other person until they are able to use their own limbs again if they recover, or feeding them forever in this way if they fail to regain the use of their limbs. If the person is mortally wounded, however, and the only way to keep them alive is by constantly doing CPR on them, then after a reasonable amount of time we would say it is okay to "let the person go." That is a silly illustration for such a serious issue, but hopefully it helps to explain where we stand. It is true that Ms. Schiavo needed someone or something to feed her and keep up with her hygiene, but her body was living on its own in the most important sense of the word. Pulling the plug on someone who is only being kept alive by a machine seems biblically appropriate, whereas starving someone to death whose body keeps itself alive and only requires external help for sustenance seems inappropriate.

(Legal) Immigration

In a sentence, those with a biblical worldview are huge fans of (legal) immigration. There is a biblical reason and a historical reason that we support allowing controlled but constant levels of immigration from other countries.

Both the Old and New Testaments have instructions about either allowing foreigners into your country, or about treating them well. For example, through Moses, God commanded the original Israelites to treat immigrants well:

> When a stranger sojourns with you in your land, you shall not do him wrong. You shall treat the stranger who sojourns with you as the native among you, and you shall love him as yourself, for you were strangers in the land of Egypt: I am the LORD your God (Lev. 19:33–34).

People from other countries are not to be considered our enemies unless they have explicitly defined themselves as such. Once an immigrant is in America, we have every obligation to treat them as we would like to be treated. Some, of course, have a problem with immigration as a concept and therefore with the immigrants themselves, because they feel as though these people are bringing America down in some way. If you feel as though immigrants are competing with citizens for limited resources in some way, then it becomes much easier to oppose them. And that is the point at which we turn to history.

Without question, one thing which has made America such a powerful and prosperous nation is the fact that we are a country of immigrants. The new ideas, constant influx of young workers, different natural skill sets, and diverse sets of local knowledge brought to the US by immigrants has had as much to do with the country we became as did our Christian heritage, democratic values, or natural resources. Economic history has proven time and again that immigrants do not take jobs away from native-born workers, but rather expand the economy so that there are more jobs for everybody. When a family moves from another country, they need a place to live and a way to heat that home, transportation, food to eat, clothes to wear, etc. American workers can then earn a living providing these essentials of life to the immigrants.

History is now also showing us those countries which have turned to capitalism all prospered initially, but vary in their longer-term results. One of the driving factors in this divide is the level of immigration. Some of the most economically successful nations in history, such as Japan and France, have seen their birthrates go down as their economic prosperity went up. Because they have not had friendly policies toward immigration and do not assimilate their immigrants into society very well, these countries are facing a glut of retired workers on government pensions—and a frightening shrinkage of younger workers to keep the economy vibrant and fund the government with tax payments. All countries will face shortages such as this to some degree, but America's challenge on this front will be minor compared to countries such as Japan, China, and most of Western Europe due to nothing more than our acceptance of immigrants looking for a better life.

A number of evangelical leaders have taken a position on the issue of immigration and the laws which govern it in the USA. They have created and signed the Evangelical Statement of Principles for Immigration Reform. It does not address the level of immigration or specific remedies for illegal immigration, but only encourages elected officials to consider what effects any laws passed or measures enforced will have on families and not just on individual immigrants. Our belief in the Bible does not provide any specifics regarding the detail of immigration law, but it does remind us to be open to the process of immigration and personally accepting of the immigrants themselves.

Interracial Relationships

This is not the controversial social topic that it used to be but, as with many other topics, there have been a number of non-Christians who have isolated and misquoted certain passages from the Bible to make it appear as tough God has forbidden individuals of different races or ethnic backgrounds to marry. If we simply look at all the Scriptures related to the topic, we can quickly see that this is not the case. The verses used out of context related to interracial marriage are quoted below:

- Observe what I command you this day. Behold, I will drive out before you the Amorites, the Canaanites, the Hittites, the Perizzites, the Hivites, and the Jebusites. Take care, lest you make a covenant with the inhabitants of the land to which you go, lest it become a snare in your midst. You shall tear down their altars and break their pillars and cut down their Asherim (for you shall worship no other god, for the LORD, whose name is Jealous, is a jealous God), lest you make a covenant with the inhabitants of the land, and when they whore after their gods and sacrifice to their gods and you are invited, you eat of his sacrifice, and you take of their daughters for your sons, and their daughters whore after their gods and make your sons whore after their gods (Ex. 34:11–16).

- When the LORD your God brings you into the land that you are entering to take possession of it, and clears away many nations before you, the Hittites, the Girgashites, the Amorites, the Canaanites, the Perizzites, the Hivites, and the Jebusites, seven nations more numerous and mightier than you, and when the LORD your God gives them over to you, and you defeat them, then you must devote them to complete destruction. You shall make no covenant with them and show no mercy to them. You shall not intermarry with them, giving your daughters to their sons or taking their daughters for your sons, for they would turn away your sons from following me, to serve other gods. Then the anger of the LORD would be kindled against you, and he would destroy you quickly (Deut. 7:1– 4).

It should be obvious from those verses that what God is forbidding is for His followers to intermarry with individuals who practice certain religions which are hostile to Him, and the true religion that He is establishing for them. God does not tell His followers that they cannot intermarry with anybody of a different race; He only forbids their marrying people of seven specific races (all of which practiced religions that we know had pretty disgusting practices). But there are verses which make the same point even more directly:

And I will set your border from the Red Sea to the Sea of the Philistines, and from the wilderness to the Euphrates, for I will give the inhabitants of the land into your hand, and you shall drive them out before you. You shall make no covenant with them and their gods. They shall not dwell in your land, lest they make you sin against me; for if you serve their gods, it will surely be a snare to you (Ex. 23:31–33).

Of course, one way to make sure that God was not forbidding all interracial marriages (and to stay true to the best methods of biblical interpretation) is to examine the Scriptures to see if there are any instances when God approved of individuals of different races marrying. And it turns out that God actually provided the rules His followers should adhere to in that regard, in various verses found in Deuteronomy 20–21. The rules seem weird to us today (nifty little guidelines such as if you see a foreign woman you want to marry, bring her home, shave her head, and wait a month before you take her as your wife), but the point is that God did not disapprove of marriages between people from different ethnic backgrounds.

All the verses quoted above were from the Old Testament, more than a thousand years before Jesus. However, a search of the New Testament reveals the same principles—that is, that there are no restrictions on dating or marrying people of a different race, but that those who are followers of Jesus Christ should avoid dating and marrying individuals who are not themselves followers of Christ: "Do not be unequally yoked with unbelievers. For what partnership has righteousness with lawlessness? Or what fellowship has light with darkness?" (2 Cor. 6:14).

Boycotts

This is an area of much conversation and disagreement within the evangelical community. Though we all try to avoid buying products such as men's magazines (which we believe portray women as only objects to be used by men for pleasure), or watching movies with actual sexual scenes in them or paying to have abortions performed, the way we interact with the companies who make those products but also make non-offensive products is much more difficult to navigate.

This issue seemed to arise almost as soon as there was a Christian community. One example discussed in the Scriptures is whether it is right or wrong to eat meat sold in the marketplace which came from animals that were sacrificed by non-Christian religious officials to idols. A number of the early Christians were poor, and meat from animals that had been sacrificed in pagan temples to pagan gods could be easily and cheaply bought in the marketplace in a number of places in those days. There were really a couple of questions being debated. First, should a consumer even ask whether the meat in question had come from an animal sacrificed in a non-Christian religious ceremony, or should products be purchased in the marketplace without knowledge or regard to their origin (the first argument over a "don't ask, don't tell" policy!). The second question was whether it is bad for a Christian to purchase from a business which would likely take the money earned and reinvest it in some non-Christian practice. The apostle Paul writes about such issues in more than one book in the New Testament. He seems to say that it is more a matter of each individual's conscience and that there are no hard right and wrongs in matters such as these. For example:

> For the kingdom of God is not a matter of eating and drinking but of righteousness and peace and joy in the Holy Spirit. . . . The faith that you have, keep between yourself and God. Blessed is the one who has no reason to pass judgment on himself for what he approves. But whoever has doubts is condemned if he eats, because the eating is not from faith. For whatever does not proceed from faith is sin (Rom. 14:17, 22–23).

The issue hit the shores of America with full force during the late years of the anti-slavery movement. Both black and white Christian leaders in that initiative began to encourage people in the northern states, and governments and consumers in European countries, to boycott products from the southern states (such as cotton and tobacco). They pressed that neither the raw materials nor any finished product made from raw materials worked on by slaves be purchased. Their arguments against trading with the southern states, of course, were based on issues of biblical moral conscience. "How can we support the businesses of plantation owners who work and abuse fellow humans against their will?" Those who opposed such boycotts generally had logic which ran along these lines: If a poor child (who could be black) in the north can purchase a thick jacket for the winter instead of risking their life wearing only thin shirts because the jackets are so much cheaper made with plentiful southern cotton, how do I tell them it is morally wrong?

Questions such as these are never easy to answer. Some Christian groups have tried to take a firm stance on such issues but quickly discover the devil really can be in the details. Of course, Christians are opposed to companies which exploit women as only sex objects, and those which produce material that is offensive or harmful to children. Beyond those basic categories, which many Americans are opposed to in one way or another, Christians will also avoid companies when they think the companies are not treating their employees well, using deceptive advertising, or have been cited by the government for fraudulent activities (price fixing, etc.).

Most decisions about which companies to patronize and which to avoid, though, are made person-to-person, based on individual conscience. In the groups of evangelicals that I have spent time with, there does seem to be some overlap in the companies which we trade with and those which we try to avoid. But there is no biblical mandate that we avoid companies managed by atheists, or that we buy only products explicitly produced to glorify God.

Though the Bible doesn't provide direct revelation on every issue we face in modern-day America, the examples above show that it does have commandments and practical advice on hundreds of current topics. Christians should search their Bibles and build an understanding of how God guides us in these areas, always avoiding the temptation to read into the Scriptures what we want or think should be there instead. Christians must also continue to resist the pressure to conform to the latest social and cultural trends and fads, if they are unbiblical.

CHAPTER 9

The View of the Church's Challenges

Religion, broadly defined, has a number of outstanding issues and challenges. My goal in this chapter, however, is not to speak about all religions, churches, or denominations. I am specifically addressing the issues of those who hold to the biblical view of the world. Within the Bible-believing community, there are a number of common challenges. Some of these challenges are as old as Christianity itself, and we need to be aware of them because they pop back up from time to time; a few others are specific to the Bible-based church in the modern age. In this chapter, I will quickly touch on seven issues that holding a biblical view suggests are challenges facing Bible-believing Christians and their churches today.

1. Unity among Bible-Believing Christians and Churches

As Rick Deighton has noted in his book *Ready to Give an Answer*, in the last prayer that Jesus spoke on earth before He was arrested and crucified, He prayed for His people to be unified as a body of believers, while adhering to the truth of the words in the Bible (John 17:17–23). For Jesus to have made the issue of unity the last thing He prayed about on earth clearly shows how important it was to Him, and gives us a hint that He was concerned it would be an issue for His followers going forward.

And boy has it been an issue! As Deighton points out, Jesus did not want His people to forsake or compromise the truth in order to just get along with everybody, but He obviously wants us to work as hard as we can with those who place the same level of importance on the Bible to stay unified despite other petty differences. There was a movement referred to as the Restoration Movement in America—fueled by Methodist, Baptist, and Presbyterian ministers—which started in the early 1800s with the intention of unifying Christ's church. Today, however, that movement has split into three main bodies, with various subfactions among them. The splits occurred over organ music, how many cups communion is served in, etc. Sad!

Jesus does not want us to compromise on the truth. If compromise were acceptable, Christ might have compromised His way out of death on a cross. But there is a disturbing and hideously sinful lack of unity among the people of earth who boldly claim that the Bible *is* truth. It is unacceptable, and every Christian with a biblical worldview—especially every Christian leader and teacher with a biblical worldview—should strive, *literally* every day, to achieve a greater level of unity among Bible-believing Christians and churches, in the US and across the globe. As teachers and leaders in churches know, they will be judged by a strict standard (James 3:1) on issues such as whether they taught the truth unadulterated by man's opinions or traditions, and whether they promoted unity or settled for (or even promoted) division.

This first issue is directly related to my second challenge.

2. Defending Our Denomination's Doctrine vs. Searching the Bible for Truth

I had a conversation recently with a Bible-college graduate who made the following comment: "It seems as though the professors spent more time teaching me to defend their version of Christian doctrine than they did instructing me in how to systematically derive biblical truth from the text." There are two tightly interrelated dimensions to this issue.

When it comes to human knowledge, such as our scientific understanding of the natural world, mistakes are made that have to be reexamined and corrected; and new learnings have to be added to the existing knowledge that has stood the test of time. Therefore, in those endeavors, it is useful to study the hypotheses and discoveries of the thought leaders who have come before. But the Bible is truth. Therefore, it can be harmful to put too much emphasis on what those who have come before say the Bible means.

Of course, studying the construct of the Hebrew and Greek languages in which the Bible was originally written greatly aids our direct study of the text, as does building an understanding of Jewish culture in antiquity. But taking an interpretation of the Bible from some scholar who lived centuries ago—and exerting more energy in defending *their* views than in developing our own views from a diligent self-study of the Scriptures—is a concern for Christians and churches today. Whether in small, informal Bible studies at the local coffee shop or graduate-level classes at the most prestigious seminaries, more time should be put into taking systematic, fresh looks into the Scriptures for the eternal truths that exist there than time spent studying the doctrines of the so-called "church fathers." Francis Chan, the author of the bestselling book *Crazy Love*, is a big proponent of this line of thinking as well, encouraging himself and other Christians to read the Bible openly, rather than only taking their doctrine from what they have been taught by others.

The closely related second dimension is that besides those who came before us in interpreting the Scriptures being themselves susceptible to errors, we can plainly see with hindsight that the time and circumstances in which they lived and worked (for example, historical periods where Protestant scholars were struggling to beat back erroneous precepts coming from the Catholic Church) sometimes had too great an influence on some of the doctrines they have pulled from the Word. We have to be careful not to let the time and circumstances we find ourselves in influence what we believe (or want to believe) the Bible has to say. And we have to be equally cautious not to too eagerly accept the view of others who may have been subject to external influences.

For example, if you had no prior knowledge of anything related to Christianity or the various traditions of different denominations and looked only at the Bible (in the words of Francis Chan: if you were stranded on an island, with only the Bible), I do not believe you would derive any of the following ideas based on the text itself (and this is just a small sample):

- *What is commonly referred to as the Sinner's Prayer.* It's unclear exactly where this originated but likely gained popularity (intentionally or unintentionally) as a way to speed up converting large groups of people to the faith with minimal effort on the part of those delivering the gospel message. But the message that we see Jesus and His followers (John the Baptist, Peter, Paul, etc.) employing was a bit different than the form the Sinner's Prayer takes today. David Platt, the aforementioned author of the bestselling book *Radical,* stated something similar at a conference in 2012 and it, unfortunately, created quite a controversy.

- *The idea that addictions such as those to drugs and alcohol are diseases.* This line of thinking came from the nonreligious world but has been adopted (without biblical justification) by the majority of Bible-believing Christians. Not all of those in the secular world agree that these addictions are a disease; the leading academic who argues against such a view is Stanton Peele, Ph.D., J.D., one of the leading researchers in the field of addiction. I believe the Bible teaches that man's bent toward sin is the "disease," and that our addictions are just one of many symptoms.

- *Infant baptism.* This is drawn from a Catholic tradition. Nothing in the Bible even remotely points to such a practice (the argument that it replaces circumcision—which is not a biblical argument—was formulated after the fact to justify the practice once it existed). If one read the Bible cover to cover today and had no other influences on their opinion, they would never dream of such a doctrine.

- *The dismissal of the need for believer's baptism.* The aforementioned Francis Chan created a stir when he commented that he believes the Bible teaches we are to repent and be baptized. I do not believe one could read the New Testament and honestly say that it is *not* calling for those who come to faith in Christ to repent and be baptized. But many denominational leaders essentially see "repent" and "baptized" as negative words. All those who believe in the sanctity of Scripture must do all they can to ensure that their beliefs come from those Scriptures, doing an honest inventory of what is truth and what is tradition.

3. The Treatment of Those Inside vs. Outside the Body of Believers

The church has to always remain vigilant against being too critical of those outside the Christian faith for not living the way the Bible calls us to, while also remaining vigilant against being too accommodating of those inside the church who are not adhering to those biblical guidelines. It is human nature to rally the troops and defend those who are like us, while seeking to condemn those who are different from and/ or directly oppose us. Of course, New Testament churches and their members are to preach repentance to nonbelievers, but the Bible teaches that we are to do it "with complete patience and teaching" (2 Tim. 4:2). Read the words of Paul from his letter to the church at Corinth, and it is clear what the Bible teaches on this issue:

> I wrote to you in my letter not to associate with sexually immoral people—not at all meaning the sexually immoral of this world, or the greedy and swindlers, or idolaters, since then you would need to go out of the world. But now I am writing to you not to associate with anyone who bears the name of brother if he is guilty of sexual immorality or greed, or is an idolater, reviler, drunkard, or swindler—not even to eat with such a one. For what have I to do with judging outsiders? Is it not those inside the church whom you are to judge? God judges those outside. "Purge the evil person from among you" (1 Cor. 5:9–13).

Simply put, God is telling us not to pick on someone outside the church if they have not agreed that they want to live by God's rules— just keep encouraging them to give themselves over to God and agree to live by His rules. If they choose to never give their lives to God, then God Himself will judge them for it. But for those who have made a public confession of faith, we are not to just look past their egregious sins, because they are now our brothers and sisters in Christ.

4. Making Decisions Based on Social Pressure and Not on the Bible

An area where Bible-believing Christians and churches must remain ever-vigilant is in not letting public and social pressure determine what we support and what we do not. The Bible—not the ever-changing opinions of man—is our guiding source. For example, centuries went by with all the known world supporting slavery—and with those who stuck to the Bible's guidance being ridiculed for claiming that these innocent Africans deserved the same shot at life as everyone else. The social and political pressure was immense, and too many Christians who otherwise had a biblical worldview grew silent or adjusted their view on the topic. Eventually, of course, everyone else came around to our point of view, and slavery is almost universally condemned today.

In the current age, the top issue is abortion. Our biblical standing is the same—those innocent humans deserve the same shot at life as everyone else. And, just as before, the political and social pressure is strongly against our view. But we must continue to defend the defenseless, regardless of whether our stand is currently popular or not.

But abortion is not the only area. Fads come and go with the intellectual and societal elite groups, who obsess over having the moral approval of their peers. Before Christians jump on the latest (but probably short-lived) trend, we just need to make sure the ideas are biblical, and not let others pressure or sway our thinking in a way we will regret later.

5. Striking the Right Balance Between Acceptance and Commitment in Preaching and Teaching

A never-ending challenge for the church is in striking the right balance between following Paul's example of "I have become all things to all people, that by all means I might save some" (1 Cor. 9:22b) and preaching the commitment message of Jesus: "And he said to all, 'If anyone would come after me, let him deny himself and take up his cross daily and follow me'" (Luke 9:23). Churches must continue to be accessible and creative with the message of the gospel. We have to meet people where they are, and give them compelling reasons to listen to our message about reconciliation with God through Christ. But we cannot preach costless conversions to a cheap and easy faith. Christ requires true repentance—an honest desire to walk away from sin, and to give leadership of your life over to Him. As the verse from Luke captures, this has a cost—self-denial, and deliberately taking up one's cross *every day.*

Christians reading this are probably saying, "We know that." And we do. But if I had to pick one area where churches seem to be conveniently blind to being out of biblical balance, it would be on this issue. (Please do not think I claim to stand innocent pronouncing judgment on others. I have been involved in church leadership long enough to have tipped the scales out of balance in both directions.) Humans have an amazing ability to rationalize what we do. Christians who are working for the growth of God's earthly kingdom have the ultimate ready-made excuse for why they need to do things the way they are doing them. My challenge here is for churches to remain cognizant that the balance often tips—from being too lax in teaching Christians what is truly required to be followers of Christ, to being too rigid and not open enough to those in the world who need Christ the most.

6. The Danger of Becoming Too Committed to a Single Political Party

As mentioned in chapter 4, when armed with an understanding of the biblical view of man, Christians should know better than to support only a single political party. I understand that the issues of slavery and abortion have driven many believers into the "religious right." But I must repeat here that I think this is a very real challenge for today's church. We should endeavor to be involved with and influence both parties, within the limits of our individual consciences.

Biblical principles stress to us that no one person and no one party will be correct about everything all the time. The biblical worldview of Christians teaches us to value the input we can gather from various sources for counsel, as we participate in political debate and decisions. Russell Moore with the Southern Baptist Convention is another evangelical leader sounding this trumpet. For details about his concerns relative to this and related issues, see "Can the Religious Right Be Saved?" in the January 2017 edition of *First Things*.

7. The Danger of Too Much Focus on End-Times Prophecy

The apostle Peter tells us that the purpose of our understanding, and of being reminded that this world will end when Jesus comes back, is so that we will be encouraged to live the type of life Jesus calls us to in the meantime (2 Peter 3). The book of Revelation seems to have been primarily written to encourage believers, over all ages of time, that Jesus ultimately wins and Satan ultimately loses. The opening verse of Revelation says that God wanted to use the book to show believers what was beginning to take place as the church started its march through history. Revelation does not seem to be written in a linear fashion from beginning to end. For example, there is an account of all sorts of events to take place during the New Testament church era that Jesus established when He left the earth in the first eleven chapters of the book; yet, in the twelfth chapter of Revelation, there is a retelling of the birth of Jesus. The book seems to deal with cycles of church strength and adherence to the Bible, followed by persecution from political forces and rising pressure from false religions, of revivals in the belief and courage of the followers of Jesus, and their ensuing seduction by social and economic forces (for further reading on this approach to understanding Revelation, consider William Hendriksen's book *More Than Conquerors*). It is not written as a time-scale which can only be decoded by the most learned and faithful Christians in order to decipher special knowledge about the end of times. In fact, Jesus directly warns us that none of us will know the day or the hour when He is to return, and so we should not focus on it. He will return, as He said, "like a thief in the night" (1 Thess. 5:2), and our concern is to be how we are living when it happens.

God knew it would be helpful to remind His followers that He ultimately wins, so that we are encouraged to press on even in the darkest of days. And He knew it would be helpful to remind us of all the political, economic, social, and false religious temptations we would need to be prepared to endure as they ebb and flow throughout history. But in today's churches there has been a growing obsession with end-times predictions; discussions of a single Antichrist; and sermons, books, and movies about a rapture. It is critical to point out that the word "rapture" is not in the Bible, and that not every dedicated believer interprets the letters to the Thessalonians or the book of Revelation as predicting a rapture at all. This one view—that, seven years before Jesus comes back, believers on the earth will go up in a "secret" ascension before mass tribulation hits the earth directed by a single Antichrist—has taken too much of a hold on evangelical churches today, in my opinion. Nowhere does the Bible instruct us to focus so much on these topics. I think Bible-believers have gotten too far off the rails on this topic. In addition to it lacking true biblical justification, I see two other issues with this.

First, some who hold positions of authority and persuasion in large, modern churches are beginning to claim that their interpretation is the only correct way to view how the end-times will unfold. It is leading them to spend as much time teaching people the signs of the end of times, and ways to identify the Antichrist and avoid getting the mark of the beast, as they do teaching people to evangelize the lost or to beware of their own bent for sin and their need to grow more like Christ each day. The truth is, we are not exactly sure how the end times will unfold.

Though they need to encourage the flock, church leaders do not need to be taking their congregation's eyes off of evangelism and spiritual growth, or setting false expectations about current and future events among the public. One of the main reasons that the Jewish people of Jesus' time rejected Him as their king is because the religious leaders of the day had a fixed idea in their minds of how the coming of the

Messiah would occur, based on their interpretations of the Old Testament Scriptures. Churches do not need to repeat that mistake today.

The second issue is that some evangelical leaders have made—and more appear to be on the verge of making—"false" predictions about when the rapture they believe in will occur and the world will actually end. I put "false" in quotes because they are too savvy to make a prediction of a single point in time (remember, according to Moses and Jesus, false predictions are the main identifier of a religion that isn't true). Rather, they make statements such as "within a generation—usually counted as sixty years—after Israel becomes a nation again, Jesus will call us home." The individuals who originally made such statements have essentially been proven wrong, as the sixty-year point passed in May 2008. Others are saying that it will be within a generation of Israel rebuilding a temple in its previous place in Jerusalem, etc. But none of those statements are in the Bible. Scriptures have to be interpreted a bit loosely and/or inconsistently to draw those exact conclusions.

If the obsession with all things related to the end of times is so fraught with negative issues, why do modern churches and their leaders seem to so readily wallow in the muddy doctrines of the rapture, the Antichrist, Armageddon, etc.? There is always a temptation with every group to have some undisclosed knowledge and/or special benefits that accrue only to members. Therefore, it is tempting to Christians and their leaders to hold dear the idea that we know something others do not and/or that we will be treated differently than others will be treated. But Christ tells us that this normal human outlook is not to be our attitude. We are simply to roll with the flow, distinguishing ourselves by our (biblical) love for others and being God's earthly ambassadors.

Another direct influence on the rising importance of end-times subjects is simply the popularity that the topic continues to enjoy. Each new book or movie about a rapture or an Antichrist seems to generate more interest than what came before. Every teen and young-adult class I have ever been involved with has wanted to study the topic. Wanting to understand how the future is going to unfold is a natural desire within most of us, and so teaching and preaching on the subject can certainly draw a crowd. The more books that are sold, and the more crowds drawn, the more difficult it gets to honestly reassess whether the doctrine is correct—and/or whether it is, correct or not, being given too much press and pulpit attention.

I believe it would be best if churches today reevaluated how they interpret the book of Revelation. But I am certain that it would be best if they placed less emphasis on end-times prophecies all together.

Any organization made up of human beings will have its challenges and faults. It is critical, however—given the important role the church plays in society—that we continually reground ourselves in the truth of Scripture. Jesus ridiculed the religious leaders of his day because they had replaced the commandments of God with the traditions of men. That is an ongoing threat for us today as well. Through the ages, the specifics of what the church is challenged with have changed; however, the underlying threat has remained constant—the tendency to drift away from what is written in the Word of God, either by being overly impacted by social influences or by relying too much on traditions.

CHAPTER 10

The View of America's Challenges

In this final chapter, I will focus on five issues which appear to be some of America's biggest challenges when viewed through the lens of the Bible. It is important to note that these are not my personal opinions or a list of my pet peeves (anyone interested in those can drop me a line). As this book has made plain, the Bible sets out a consistent and broad-reaching view of the world for those who believe it to be the authoritative word of God. The Bible is timeless and has proven to be perfectly accurate. We all have our ideas of what we would like to see America become, and the endeavors we wish our great country would cease or take up. Many of those items are based on emotion, personal opinion, or ephemeral whims. The challenges below, however, are those which an objective view of the Scriptures would suggest America must prepare herself to address.

1. The Ever-Growing Threat to Free Speech and Open Debate

Some of the most disturbing headlines in this regard have occurred in just the last few years—for example, the IRS being under congressional scrutiny for unfairly (most say illegally) targeting certain types of non-profit organizations with whose politics they disagreed, distinguished speakers such as Condoleezza Rice not being allowed to speak at public institutions of higher learning, and Ayaan Hirsi Ali ultimately being denied the honorary degree she was offered by Brandeis University because those in control disagreed with her views and opinions. This trend is one of the biggest threats America has ever faced. Christians would never try and silence the speech of someone like Hirsi Ali, especially on a university campus, even though she is an atheist.

It has already been stated many times in these pages that the Bible teaches us no one is perfect all the time, and that we need to consider the counsel and advice of a broad range of people to ensure we are making the best decisions. This absolutely holds for those in government. A few Bible verses which point to this fact are:

- Where there is no guidance, a people falls, but in an abundance of counselors there is safety (Prov. 11:14).
- The way of a fool is right in his own eyes, but a wise man listens to advice (Prov. 12:15).
- Without counsel plans fail, but with many advisers they succeed (Prov. 15:22).
- Plans are established by counsel; by wise guidance wage war (Prov. 20:18).

The biblical filter through which I see the world teaches me that the greater value is in the concept of open debate facilitated by free speech—much more so than in either the concepts of conservative or liberal governance. Believing in and supporting free speech is considerably more important than being a Republican or Democrat! Some individuals become absolutely convinced, however, that they are correct and therefore do not see a problem with shutting down the free speech of others with whom they disagree. If you are only silencing falsehood or errors, then what is the harm, they ask? Others seem less convinced of their own infallibility, but develop such a hatred for those whose views differ from theirs that they seem to relish the idea of clamping down on the communication of their foes.

Let me state it again: The value of free speech, and the benefit of open and honest debate and disagreement, far outweighs the advantage to be realized—even by the best political thought leaders, with the sincerest attitudes, gaining an unobstructed monopoly in the communications arena. I am not sure how to convince all my fellow Americans, but I am quite convinced myself that putting even the elementary limits on free speech which some in this country have begun to do will not provide the long-term results they desire. When free speech is curtailed, eventually all parts of society suffer—even those who thought they were ultimately protecting their version of the truth. For the point of view on this issue from a political liberal with a biblical understanding, read Kristen Powers' *The Silencing: How The Left Is Killing Free Speech*.

2. Our National Debt, and Federal and State Unfunded Liabilities

Just as there are proverbs about the value of free speech and open debate, there are as many or more regarding the danger of (too much) debt. A sampling of such verses is below.

- Whoever puts up security for a stranger will surely suffer harm, but he who hates striking hands in pledge is secure (Prov. 11:15).
- The rich rules over the poor, and the borrower is the slave of the lender (Prov. 22:7).
- Be not one of those who give pledges, who put up security for debts (Prov. 22:26).

The problem with a writer such as myself trumpeting the dangers of our nation having too much debt is that there have been so many books warning about this issue over the past thirty or so years that it has lost almost all of its sting. The problem is that these past warnings were people "crying wolf." These authors knew they were crying wolf, but their readers did not. When I was an undergraduate in college, everyone from Ivy League economists to government bureaucrats were writing books about how the deficits the nation was running under President Reagan were going to cause our national debt to skyrocket, which in turn was going to cause inflation and interest rates to shoot back up, destroying the economy. Of course, this didn't happen. And as I have stated, the sad thing is the authors knew that these outcomes were not going to occur. They disagreed with Reagan's economic platform and shamelessly cried wolf, as children pitch a temper tantrum when not getting their way. This dynamic makes it much more difficult to bring this issue to the forefront and address it effectively. People say, "We have heard this before and, frankly, the warnings which never materialize are growing old."

But the problem is that both our national debt (what America owes her creditors, based on the accumulation of previous budget deficits) and the unfunded liabilities of our national, state, and local governments (mostly promises we have made about pension payments and insurance coverage to those who will soon be retiring—the cost of which we have no realistic way of covering) will at some point reach crisis levels. Some city and county governments (Detroit, and Jefferson County in Alabama, for example) have already filed for bankruptcy. It should be noted that the federal government technically cannot go bankrupt, but that doesn't mean that we won't end up at some point in the foreseeable future where the interest payments we owe are greater than the tax revenue we are collecting, or where the payments we have promised to private retirees through Social Security and government retirees through their pension plans will be greater than the tax revenues we are annually taking in.

The national debt level of the United States has tripled in the last dozen years. It took the US more than two hundred years to accumulate a debt level of around six trillion dollars, and yet we have added an additional 12 trillion to it in just the last twelve years! This alone is a trend that we cannot continue. But it is also shocking to see the growth of unfunded liabilities we are stacking up at every level of government (and sad the accounting sleight-of-hand the federal government uses in order to mask these liabilities and keep them from public discussion). Economic history is full of examples (including modern-day examples in Europe and Central and South America) of countries who have suffered financial ruin based on debt levels that were too high and unfunded liabilities which were ignored for too long. This is a real issue. America is a great country, but we are not invincible—and we are certainly not above the simple rules of accounting.

I am not at all saying the US will hit a single tipping point and collapse. But I am saying the drag on our economic growth and vitality will get greater and greater, imposing in some cases irreversible consequences. The American people need to demand a strategic proposal from our elected leaders on how the country is going to honestly address these issues, and our elected government officials need to deal with the financial problems they have helped create, instead of kicking the can down the line a few more years.

3. Elected Officials Not Living in the Same System, nor Playing by the Same Rules, as the Rest of Us

I believe one thing that contributes to the challenge listed immediately above is the fact that those in the US Congress (both representatives and senators) live in a dream world of sorts that has become too disconnected from the average citizen whom they claim to represent. The approval rating for national representative and senators hovers in only the mid-teens, according to such sites as Rasmussen Reports and Real Clear Politics. That is simply abysmal. In the 2016 presidential primaries, candidates such as Donald Trump and Bernie Sanders gained their initial traction off this issue. But instead of being ashamed of this fact and working to get closer to the people to regain their trust and respect, those in Congress continue to isolate themselves from ordinary citizens.

Those in Congress do not share the same retirement system with the rest of us. No Social Security for them. They do not deal with Obamacare for their health insurance in the same manner that my neighbor and I do. And their retirement pensions are out of sight, to boot. This is clearly unbiblical, as the Good Book calls for leaders to think of themselves as servant leaders who are never to use their positions for their own advantage.

The longer a governing body is detached in these ways from the people they govern, the less effectively they can govern—and, to be honest, the less they care about governing well. The issue becomes even more severe if the people in question are narcissistic or egocentric (and I'm not sure that people in the entertainment industry are more narcissistic or egocentric than our national politicians). Most incumbent politicians can get reelected, though, without living by the same rules as the rest of us, and this eliminates the primary motivation they have for changing.

Americans should demand that all national politicians use the same retirement, healthcare, and education systems that we are forced to use. We need to force politicians to quit using their positions to their advantages, and we need to stop reelecting any of those who refuse to vote for such changes.

4. Sexism

I made an informal bet with a gentleman back in 2000 that a black man would become president in America before a female would. I stated that sexism was as large an issue today as racism. He was stunned that I would make such a claim, and maybe some of you readers are as well. With the election of Barack Obama to the highest office in the land (twice), at least I won the bet.

I don't claim that racism does not exist in this country. In fact, in the conversations that I have had with people while traveling across the country, it appears that about forty percent of the support for abortion is a purely racist play. One guy told me straight up that since blacks have abortions at 3.5 times the rate of whites—and that research had proven that since blacks were allowed unfettered access to abortion, crime rates in America had fallen—there was no reason to outlaw abortions now. And as others have begun to notice recently, Hollywood is quite the racist stronghold.

But I put sexism over racism in this list because at its very foundation America now knows that racism is wrong, has a common definition of what it is, and has made some very impressive attempts to erase it. And as racist as Hollywood might be, it is much more sexist! There has not been any level of agreement that sexism is a major issue in this country, how to define it, or any honest attempts to eradicate it. For example, if a commentator on a public stage makes even a mildly racist remark, their career may well be finished. If a white person used a racial slur, their career would definitely be done. But if a male comedian calls out a female by some sexist slur or refers to her as a female body part, they are celebrated. If a commentator speaks only about how a female looks, there is no backlash. Why?

I am not calling for what some label gender equality. There are natural, biological differences between men and women, and those who claim there are not come across as flat-out goofy. Women are biologically designed to carry unborn children to term, to bond with the newborn babies through the greater release of chemicals in their blood after birth, and to nurse babies. I am not suggesting that we need to figure out how men can start having babies, and I am not calling for an equal representation of women on the front lines of battle in foreign wars. That type of equality is unnatural and nonsensical. But why in America do we think it is okay to see women as primarily (or only) sexual objects who exist only for the pleasure of men?

In my travel and informal surveys, I have found that another forty percent of the support for abortion in this country seems to come from men who want a foolproof safety net in case some woman with whom they are having sex, but care nothing about, gets pregnant. It is as sad as it is shocking how women today will accept the horrible maltreatment from the men in their lives—even women who are well educated, rich, and famous. When society as a whole reinforces negative stereotypes about your self-worth as a person, I guess you can begin to believe it yourself.

Let me go to the Bible to give you a sense of how I believe women are to be viewed:

> She considers a field and buys it; with the fruit of her hands she plants a vineyard. She dresses herself with strength and makes her arms strong. She perceives that her merchandise is profitable. Her lamp does not go out at night. She puts her hands to the distaff, and her hands hold the spindle. She opens her hand to the poor and reaches out her hands to the needy. She is not afraid of snow for her household, for all her household are clothed in scarlet. She makes bed coverings for herself; her clothing is fine linen and purple. Her husband is

known in the gates when he sits among the elders of the land. She makes linen garments and sells them; she delivers sashes to the merchant. Strength and dignity are her clothing, and she laughs at the time to come. She opens her mouth with wisdom, and the teaching of kindness is on her tongue. She looks well to the ways of her household and does not eat the bread of idleness. Her children rise up and call her blessed; her husband also, and he praises her: "Many women have done excellently, but you surpass them all." Charm is deceitful, and beauty is vain, but a woman who fears the LORD is to be praised. Give her of the fruit of her hands, and let her works praise her in the gates (Prov. 31:16–31).

To paraphrase the meaning of this passage in more modern language: A woman is valuable in a business setting, though not usually as strong as a man in the physical realm, her strength in acting as a business person is not to be underestimated. And women are endowed with many more traits than just acumen in the corporate world. For example, she can also take care of her family and not just in normal times but in times of distress as well. Because of her ability to think ahead and plan for the future, she is not afraid of what lies ahead. Women not only have much to teach others but are quite skilled at it as well. Amazingly, women have all these skills and yet still show so much compassion to those who are in need, even those outside their own family or group. Women deserve to be respected by their children and flat out praised by their husbands. Oh yeah, and if you were wondering what there was to say about their physical beauty and charm, the answer is nothing. That is not how a lady is to be judged. They are not just to be thought of or used as sexual objects. Judge a woman as you would a man, by the success and value of the things that they do and the type of person they are inside.

So I ask: Why aren't male comedians, singers, producers, directors, etc., in Hollywood held accountable for incessantly promoting the view that women are primarily sexual objects to be used by men at large?

Why are male athletes who commit domestic violence (in the college or professional ranks) not held to a much stricter standard? Why on earth would it not be one strike and you are out on domestic-abuse issues? Why does the media insist that abuses (or even perceived abuses) by whites against blacks are so much more egregious than that of men against women? Why does a bitterly sexist male get a "free pass" from the politically correct police, as long as he says he supports abortion? Why are there so many young men on college campuses who say that it is okay to have sex with a young lady who has passed out from drinking because "she didn't say no to the request"?

I am not calling for the now defunct Equal Rights Amendment to be resurrected. Honestly, I am saying that as a country we need to move toward an attitude of equal respect. Sure, men are stronger on average, and only women can have babies. The differences in the sexes are real (and designed by our Creator to be such). But we can—and should—respect each other equally, giving due credit for how God made each of us.

5. Defending Those Who Are Unable to Defend Themselves

In one of his letters to a young student of his named Timothy, the apostle Paul wrote that we are to look after what he refers to as those who are "truly widows" (1 Tim. 5:3). The Bible often directed God's followers to look after orphans and widows—those who were in difficult circumstances through no fault of their own. Paul was enhancing this direction by essentially saying to first help those who are in difficult circumstances through no fault of their own, and have no way to defend themselves or no viable option for improving their lot.

Over the preceding centuries, Christians and churches have done a great deal, in other countries and in America, to improve the circumstances of those who were felt to be truly widows of their time, unable to defend themselves. I will provide four examples below, but not all the historical details concerning the triumphs of these endeavors. Each story is remarkable, however, and for the readers who are not familiar with the specifics, I would suggest books such as *What's So Great about Christianity* by Dinesh D'Souza and *The Book That Made Your*

World: How the Bible Created the Soul of Western Civilization by Vishal Mangalwadi.

- Orphans
- Slaves
- The living condition of prisoners
- The treatment of the mentally ill living in state asylums

I believe America, as a country, needs to follow the biblical advice of defending and promoting those who are "truly widows" in our society. As in all democracies, those who can vote have the strongest sway on the issues on which our governments focus. And somehow over time, American politicians have come to try and solve all problems with money, intentionally or unintentionally walking away from those that money can't easily fix. But America is too brave, too great, and too strong to do this. Both our citizens and our elected leaders must face the next generation of challenges, make the tough decisions required, and put in the effort to move the needle on these difficult tasks. Below I list what I believe are the top four "truly widow" challenges in the US today:

1. *Unborn Babies.* No one reading this wishes that their mother had aborted them in the womb, and no unborn child today would choose to be aborted. If the drive for life is this universal, we should protect the unborn. I understand that the primary way elements in American society are changed is through the ballot box. Vote in politicians who agree with your views, and have them legislate the changes in which you are interested. Centuries ago, slaves had no voice at the polls; today, neither do unborn babies. Therefore, we need to be the voice of these undefended, voiceless children. Citizens, politicians, and the courts should all be coming to the rescue of unborn lives. America is a decent country. We send aid to places thousands of miles away after natural disasters occur, and help our enemies rebuild after war. If the unborn could vote, we all know in our hearts that they would vote for

life. Therefore, as a decent nation full of good people, we should grant them that life!

2. *(Minority) Children in Failing Schools.* Unfortunately, this also comes down to those without a vote being held hostage to those who do vote. There are processes and programs—such as charter schools and vouchers for private schools—which recent studies have shown to be very effective in raising the educational attainment of children who were suffering in failing public schools. However, there are powerful political and financial forces which have a vested interest in the continuation of the public-school model—and they can outcampaign, outspend, and outvote the poor third-graders every time. Politicians in Washington DC, including our presidents, send their children to private schools. But these politicians should either address and fix the nation's failing public schools, or allow public money to be invested in charter programs—or allow it to be redistributed as vouchers, which parents can use to send their children to better private schools.

I know this is a heated issue and the data gets intentionally distorted beyond recognition, but the simple facts are that many public schools are not delivering the education we need for America's next great generation. Without this being aggressively addressed and subjected to some competition from educational alternatives, poor children in bad schools will start life at a severe disadvantage. Parents should have options, so let's move the hypocritical politicians out of the way (who send their children to private schools, but won't allow poor parents to be granted vouchers so they can do the same) and quit hamstringing our young people for the benefit of an already established group which apparently has too much power and control anyway.

The dysfunctional home life of many poor children today likely acts as a great anchor on their educational success, even greater probably than their failing schools (consider the lesson's in Paul

Tough's *How Children Succeed*). But we cannot legislate that parents stay together in a traditional family structure, that they read to their children, that they keep the home free of disruptive relatives and unnecessary quarrels, etc. With a touch of honesty combined with a slight bit of courage, however, the issue of allowing children in struggling schools to enjoy better options can be corrected with the stroke of a pen. So let's encourage (through our families, churches, etc.) parents staying together and raising their children, and let's also legislate changes in our educational systems, to give better options to struggling children in failing schools.

3. *The Mentally Ill Homeless.* This is such an incredibly difficult and sensitive issue. On one side of the ledger are those who want to protect the rights of individuals who choose not to be institutionalized or take medication every day. On the other side are those who express legitimate concern that those with severe mental illness (bipolar disorder with schizophrenia, for example) can be a danger to others if not treated properly, and should not have to suffer because they often lack the capacity to make the best decisions for themselves.

   Wherever you stand on the issue, we should all agree that creative solutions need to be devised and offered, and some difficult decisions made. There are simply too many mentally ill people living homeless in this country, too many languishing in prison cells, and too many who are causing grave harm to others. For most of us in our everyday lives, these poor souls trapped in their own heads wasting away in jail, or suffering mental and physical torment living unprotected on the streets, are in a sense "out of sight and out of mind." But the fact that we don't personally have to deal directly with the issue each day does not mean that as a country we should not address this challenge and implement a better solution than what exists today. These individuals, and the situations they are in, deserve our attention and care. They deserve the best resources and solutions our rich and powerful nation can provide. Tim Murphy, a US representative from

Pennsylvania, has proposed reforms that would be a good start in this arena. For more information on this topic, see *The Insanity Offense: How America's Failure to Treat the Seriously Mentally Ill Endangers Its Citizens* by E. Fuller Torrey.

4. *Cognitively Challenged Adults*: The issue here again is that this group of individuals, and those who are currently caring for them, have very little influence voting wise. The US has a very good social safety net for the individuals who fall into this broad category (Social Security disability, Medicaid, etc.), but money does not solve all the problems these individuals are facing. I believe the challenges here concern whether we are providing all the elements of a well-rounded life that we provide to other citizens. Too often the options available to these individuals are dictated by bureaucrats who seem to have little information regarding the situations these people find themselves in, and even less heart for administering robust solutions to those challenges, particularly if the best solution is a faith-based solution.

   The call here is that America's voters and elected leaders make themselves more aware of the issues involved with this group of individuals. If they need to be cared for in group homes (including those administered by faith-based organizations), then let's determine how to provide that solution in the most loving and effective way. If they need more intensive skills and job training than do others, then let's determine how we will make that option a reality. America's challenge here is simply to make this issue known to a broader audience and to build an increasingly large coalition of people who will actively seek to better the lives of cognitively challenged adults, even if they do not know one personally or do not directly benefit from the improvement in their lives. Rising above our own selfish interests and promoting the greater good is one of the defining characteristics of America. As a great nation, let's do it one more time.

   Whether we are working to determine the greatest challenges facing America, or to gain an understanding of the best way to raise our children or lead our government, those with a biblical worldview start with the Bible. But such a worldview is not derived only from the "thou shalt" commandments found in the Scriptures. The foundation of this worldview is the guidance the Bible provides about where we came from and why we exist. Layered on to this are the descriptions it provides about human nature—both positive and negative. Finally, the Bible teaches us initially so that we can discern inspired Scriptures and true religion from those that are false.

We must be rational agents, disqualifying failed hypotheses. We believe the Bible, because it has proven itself with its explanations and predictions—and because its method of using explanations and predictions to qualify winners from losers has been the defining tradition of human progress.

ABOUT THE AUTHOR

Andy earned his doctorate at the age of twenty-five. He has been involved in research at one of the country's national laboratories and worked for and consulted with Fortune 500 companies in the corporate world. Currently he is the senior minister at the First Christian Church of Mableton, near Atlanta, Georgia and is also the President and CEO of an analytical consulting company. He has been married to his wife, Tina, for twenty-eight years.